THE
MOONLIGHTER'S MANUAL

BY

JERRY LE BLANC

NASH PUBLISHING CORPORATION
LOS ANGELES, CALIFORNIA
1969

PREFACE

Moonlighting today is everybody's game: the housewife who baby-sits; the auto mechanic who repairs cars for others on his day off; the doctor who writes by night; or the corporation lawyer who plays drums in a band—all are moonlighters, whether for extra income, career advancement, or just to satisfy an outside interest their job does not fulfill. I mention doctor, lawyer—well, I even know an Indian chief who moonlights; he supplements his tribal tributes by serving as a tour guide. The butcher, the baker, the candlestick-maker—it is the rare man or woman today at any income level who has not felt the pressures of inflation and thought about ways of increasing income.

This book is designed for all such people. When you seek a moon-lighting job, even if extra income is your only immediate considera-tion, you are about to add a new phase to your life, and to that extent, your own satisfaction, happiness, and prosperity are going to be in-volved. This book aims to help make that phase as pleasurable and profitable as possible.

When you consider that there are more that 21,700 different regular occupations being practiced in America today, according to the most recent statistics of the U. S. Department of Labor; and when you ponder additionally that a popular weekly television show, *What's My Line*, can run year after year and into the de-cades without duplicating itself in its delineation of unusual jobs, you can appreciate the magnitude of the task in attempting to com-pile not only listings, but clear, how-to instructions for securing any meaningful number of these job possibilities.

So, this book does not pretend to be all-encompassing. It is quite selective, leaning toward representative jobs most readily available to large numbers of people in typical situations across the land. I am reminded of a visit I paid to a secret military installation somewhere in middle America. Above the console keyboard of a futuristic-looking piece of space-age machinery, someone had printed a sign that read, "Wanted—Nuclear physicist with interest in extra-terrestrial fission and fusion experiments dealing with a broad spectrum of orbital and interplanetary logistics, not devoid of political pressures. No experience necessary."! It was a laugh, of course, and although such a job example may be extreme, there is little reason, I believe, for including many career-type possibilities when the job qualifications call for long-range preparation and the positions usually dictate their own moonlighting possibilities.

If there is one overriding element in the approach recommended to moonlight job hunting, it is the stress placed on imagination, the use of. People often tell me, "There just isn't any work in my town. . ." or just, "It's impossible to find a part-time job. . .". You will not feel this way if you approach the job hunt thoughtfully, and if your interest is strong enough to commit yourself to reading this book, I can practically guarantee that you will soon find the spare-time profits you seek.

For example, one simple look at your local situation which I often suggest is the Yellow Pages of your telephone book, if only for perspective and encouragement. Take your own community's Yellow Pages and open them to "A" on the table in front of you, also take a copy of the telephone book from your nearest *larger* community. From "A" to "Z", compare them both, and write down all the products and services listed in the larger book which are not in your local book. You have just made a list of what your community needs, and filling one of these needs can solve all of your extra income problems or perhaps lead to a whole new future for you. And of the entries you bypassed, there's hardly one of the that does not hold some job possibilities or money-making prospect.

Although most of the specific work information which will unfold here required considerable research, your author is personally acquainted with the overwhelming majority of the jobs listed, either through having at some stage done the job himself, or through interviews with people all over the country who are working at them today—and profiting.

Credit for assistance and information herein should go to many, including the National Home Study Council, and most of the individual companies named in the text, but I would like to especially thank the government's Small Business Administration for its clear, valuable advice, so readily given which makes up much of the content of Chapter 7, telling how to go into business for yourself.

Happy hunting.

—Jerry LeBlanc

TABLE OF CONTENTS

Chapter 1
YOUR OUTLOOK ON JOBS

Gordon Jones is an average guy with one of the most common problems in America today—a shortage of money. It seems that his paycheck never quite seems to stretch far enough to pay all the bills and provide a few of the nice little extras we all love to spend money on: a vacation, new furniture, attractive clothing, a hobby, or just setting a few dollars aside for the future, for retirement, or for the kids' education. How do we solve a problem like that? What if you can't ask for a raise and there just don't seem to be any extra jobs around to bring in more income. There's nothing in the want ads, anyway.

Picture Gordon Jones. He is driving home from work, worrying about money. What can he do? He gets in his car, distractedly, noting with a frown the small dent in the side of his car door he keeps meaning to have fixed but never seems to get around to it. He starts up the car and drives off, his foot resting uneasily on the worn, slipping gas pedal. With distaste he notes a frayed spot on the auto upholstery. On top of that, he spies a stain on the lap of his pants. He shakes his head. The car moves through heavy traffic, but Jones barely notices the other vehicles, except for an occasional license plate. He passes an area of neat, older homes with frayed roofs and old mail boxes. Further along there is a new subdivision going up, with some homes all completed except for landscaping. Most are in the framing stage, the bare wood studs drawing off the future homes like a full-color blueprint. Already one home is inhabited, with milk bottles and a newspaper on the doorstep betraying its occupancy. There is a birdbath on the lawn.

Going through the business center to town, Jones sees the ubiquitous sign, "Notary Public," and it reminds him of the time he had to have a deed copy notarized. From some indistinguishable store pours the pleasant music of a piano recording. At a photo studio he can peer in through the drapes as a mother with child on her lap sits waiting in an upholstered chair. At the counter inside a girl is scratching her head, poring over a ledger. Most of the stores are closing now; it's that hour. A merchant locks his front door, glances securely at his burglar alarm, and whistles as he walks away.

It is still hot out. Jones, wishing he had air conditioning in his car—not to mention his home—extracts a cigarette from a package in his shirt pocket. He presses the cigarette lighter button before recalling that it doesn't work. Surprising how many little appliances stop working and never get fixed. He strikes a match instead and inhales the smoke. Money, he remembers, that was what I was worrying about. He is nearing home now and he is no closer to solving his problem that he was before he left, than yesterday, or last week. That's the way it usually happens, until a person takes some decisive action in the right direction—like reading this book.

If Jones only knew, he drove past the answer to his problem on the way home! He looked right at it. He listened to it. He put it in his pocket without ever realizing it!

Let's retrace Jones' ride, this time thinking about money and how to make it. Everybody has a few hours a day or a weekend they can devote to raising welcome cash if they only knew how to go about it.

That dent in his car. Lots of motorists have small dents like that which they never get around to fixing. Yet auto body repair shops are competing for business. Suppose a guy was to learn rough estimating or just make a deal with some body shop to go around and place their card on every auto windshield where there's an obvious potential customer. The shop would be glad to pay a commission for the business. And how about Jones' worn upholstery? He could sell seat covers in the same way—just by dropping a store's cards on the cars that need it. His worn accelerator pedal. Hundreds of cars are in the same shape. Maybe people would buy new pedals through the mail, or through a gas station to save themselves a trip to the mechanic's garage. License plate holders. You could personalize them and they'd sell like hot cakes. There's money in selling things that people need—or just want.

Oh, yes, that stain on his pants. What every town needs is a spot–removing specialist; somebody who'll know the right fluid or dry chemical to take out just about everything.

Those older homes? How many of the homeowners need a new paint job, or roof repairs, or more attractive gardening? Most people are proud of their homes and consider money spent on them a wise investment. Or just the mailboxes or house numbers; you could make a small fortune going from house to house and painting their name on their mailbox, their number on the curb, at $1 each. Or speaking of mail, how about the mail-order sales business? That new subdivision; all of those homes are going to need landscaping, shrubbery, mailboxes, light bulbs, floor cleaning, window washing, furniture, furnishings, a local business guide—scores of things, and the people who sell the goods and services, or just perform them, will be making plenty of money.

Should we go on? There's plenty more if you're alert and have the barest little know-how. Those framed homes. Pictures of them now would be invaluable to the owners after the studding, wiring, and plumbing is all covered up. Pictures of them finished would be eagerly purchased postcards—"Dear Mom, here's our new home." What about being a milkman, starting your day like a lot of athletes do, with a healthy, few-hour, profitable route? Newspaper distributor? How about casting and selling your own concrete building blocks?

Let's go on downtown. Anyone over twenty-one can earn money as a notary public, or a voter registrar, for that matter, if you know how to go about it. Music? How about selling or exchanging records or sheet music, or even tuning pianos? A photo studio? There are fortunes to be made in taking the right pictures. Drapes and upholstery? It's easy to learn drapery making and upholstering with a little guidance, or just selling the materials for drapes or recovering upholstery can be vastly profitable on a part-time basis. The girl with the books? You can't imagine how many small businesses would love to find someone to take their bookkeeping off their hands. How about selling or installing burglar alarms, or serving as a merchant patrolman?

Air conditioning is a big business today; sales, repairs, installing, thousands of people have idle on their shelves appliances like toasters, mixers, coffee percolators, lamps, tools. You don't have to be a jack-of-all trades with fix-it knowledge; you could profit from this situation by offering a service of shipping the broken articles to the manufacturer or other repairmen—for a markup, of course.

And even Jones' matches could solve his money problem; bars, businesses, hotels, manufacturers—scores of opportunities exist for quick sales of matchbook advertising at a handy profit. Consider Jones' condition; he is likely in debt, yet even debt collecting for others could get him out.

Jones is a fictitious character of course, but his plight is very real. He thinks there is a shortage of cash and a shortage of jobs. There is no shortage of jobs, no shortage of opportunity. Look around you. In the average room there are ideas for dozens of money-making opportunities. I'll give you a dozen and if you get your mind working, chances are you'll be able to list another twelve. If you can't now, you will be able to after reading only a little of this book.

Take twelve: furniture refinishing; television tube testing; floor waxing; carpet shampooing; painting pictures or framing them; making planters or artificial flowers; selling magazines, or advertising in them; replacing light fixtures; selling door chimes; fixing or installing locks, screen doors, and windows; cleaning furnaces. That's really a baker's dozen. Try the game yourself, connecting a possible money-making job with every article your eyes fall on. And then consider this: there's even more money to be made in the articles that aren't there, through sales.

So you don't like selling. Lots of people don't. So you don't have any special skills, or only one—your current job. Well, even if that is such a common skill as housekeeping, it is a service that is in demand elsewhere. If you have children, or lack transportation, or are disabled and can't leave the house, there are ways for you to make money. And some of the country's biggest salesmen never meet a customer face to face; they let someone else do the selling for them. Whether you have an hour a day or ten, there are things you can do, things you can make, talents you can put to work, small investments that pay off big, and possibly a whole new life of high income and satisfaction in doing the things you like to do.

Let's start by telling you this: this is the simplest book you have ever read, and it can be the most profitable. Don't start on the next page. Flip through until you find a chapter that interests you most, for we all work best and make the most of it when we are doing something that we like. From there, read in both directions to the back and front of the book. There are ideas you never dreamed of. Dollars waiting for you everywhere. And don't miss a word; the right part-time job for you is in this book, and it may open your eyes to a whole new life of prosperity and happiness.

Chapter 2
WORKING AT HOME

Suppose for some very good reason—either because you must care for children, lack transportation, or are a semi-invalid— you can't leave your home to seek gainful employment, and with it the apparent answer to all your money problems. Whatever you do, don't consider this a strike against yourself, a handicap. While mobility is certainly very important in the commercial world today, do you know that there are an estimated three million Americans who work at home, either full or part time, by their own choice! And millions more would love to, if they could.

As a matter of fact, working exclusively out of your home has numerous profitable advantages. From the very start of the day, for example, you don't have to pay transportation costs to work like most people do, either in the form of supporting an automobile or paying ever-rising bus and streetcar fares. And you save an hour or two hours a day by not getting involved in frustrating traffic tie-ups enroute. The person who works at home can have his or her first hour's work done, still feeling fresh, by the time the commuter arrives at work, ragged and nervous from the battle of morning rush-hour traffic.

On top of that, the woman who works at home can save on one of the biggest profit-eaters, baby-sitting costs, which often reduce a working mother's take-home pay actually to only a few dollars a day. There are other big savings, too. If you work at home you do not need to purchase an expensive wardrobe to compete with all the fashion-plate working girls, and you don't have to pay for lunches at downtown restaurant prices.

More advantages: when it comes to income tax time, by working at home you have made yourself eligible for numerous special deductions, including a percentage of the entire year's rent, light, heating, and telephone bills. If you invest in a desk, typewriter, work table, files, paper and pencils, all working equipment is tax deductible. But the biggest, sweetest break of all when it comes to working at home is this: you are your own boss.

There are a few disadvantages; let's face it. Sometimes it can be nice to get out of the house and circulate in a different scene. On the other hand, working at home doesn't exile you from society, either, does it? At home there can be many distractions: the children making noise, the telephone ringing, people coming to the door. Sometimes there is a lack of stimulation and equipment that is readily available in the atmosphere of a store, office, or factory surroundings. You may find that there are zoning restrictions or permits required, but these generally apply only to sales type operations and are neither difficult nor costly hurdles.

One point is clear from the experience of thousands who make a good living or side income at home: if you are going to work at home, you must summon up the determination to overcome the distractions and shortcomings of your employment and learn to take full advantage of the blessings of being able to perform enjoyable, money-making tasks without leaving the comforts of home. You must be a self-starter, because you will set your own hours and work only as leisurely or as hard as you like. There will never be a boss looking over your shoulder. Who is going to pay you for working in your own home when they won't be able to watch and see if you really are working? Well, actually, you will be your own boss and you will be the only one who must keep track of your efforts. Your pay, since it does not depend on your presence at some place of business, will depend on your production. So if it normally takes two hours to do a certain task, like making an object, but it takes you four hours to do it because you watch television while working, you'll find you've really only worked two hours and that's all you'll be getting paid for. Some manufacturers and offices operate in the same way: workers are paid by the hour, but if they don't produce an average number of pieces of work, whether it is a matter of letters being filed, bills being typed, or television circuits soldered, the worker soon finds his or her pay reduced or job withdrawn. You have to adjust your own time clock. But once you discover how easy and rewarding it is, and how much work you have to do at your own pace to make the extra money you need, you will find yourself choosing the best time of day and tackling your job with zest, regularly.

People will say, "Aren't you lucky, earning money at home without even going downtown!" True, in most cases you won't be making a direct exchange of an hour's work for an hour's pay on a regular weekly paycheck basis, but how does $5 an hour sound to you? Doesn't that make up for any uncertainties? No, you don't have to sell things if you don't want to. Not at all. There are many jobs which do not require selling. Somebody else does it. Read on, and you will find scores of jobs. Pick one and act! Decide today, right now, that you are going to earn the money you need to pay all your bills and spend for the enjoyment of the finer things.

The jobs listed in this chapter have one thing in common: all can be done by someone who is basically restricted to his own home. They are many and varied, and surely one of these moonlighting jobs will appeal to every person's taste as something he would like to do, even without considering the beauty of an extra income. But however broad this list, it does not have to be the limit of jobs available and does not even pretend to be all-inclusive. The fact is, there are just too many to list. Many of the jobs listed in other chapters could be at least partially adapted to homework. An imaginative person will get ideas for dozens of other money-making, interesting occupations. Read every one of them. Keep your mind open. Think positive. The answer to all your financial problems may soon pop up right in front of your eyes.

MAKE COSTUME JEWELRY

Do you like to create beautiful things? Do you take special pride in making little things like table decorations? Then perhaps you could make your fortune in even smaller items, designing and creating your own items of jewelry. Does that sound impossibly difficult? It isn't. If you like working with your hands and have a little talent for recognizing beauty, you've got what it takes. One woman who was simply passing time with a hobby of making her own earrings found she had created an item so popular that she has since expanded into a full line of nationally selling jewelry and the profits are fantastic! Think about it: is there some special small stone in your state that is rare elsewhere, like petrified wood scraps in Arizona and New Mexico, silver mine tailing rocks in Nevada, bloodstones from Oregon, jasper quartz from Texas, or even granite from Maine? How about sea shells from the Atlantic or Pacific or Gulf states? There are earring and brooch kits available which provide the basic gold-plated pin or fixture. So you affix your native polished stones or some other curious, small items like coins, miniature castings of animals, or whatever, and you have created and manufactured your own jewelry. If it's a particularly regional item like a rare local stone, you could make a dozen pairs of earrings, for example, and ask you local souvenir shop to offer them for sale to tourists. Or invest in a local newspaper or national magazine ad; but watch out, you may find yourself flooded with orders, so many that you'll be working full time instead of part time turning them out. This can be very enjoyable, very satisfying work and you can be your own first customer for every item, wearing—incidentally, advertising—lovely pieces of original jewelry. All you need is a desk drawer and a few square feet of space in your home to work, plus a few materials which usually are readily available locally. Find a local hobby shop and ask them about starter jewelry-making kits; you may soon be buying them in quantities—at a discount—and selling them quickly and easily.

Earnings

Prices will vary, but approximately, you can expect that an earring kit, for example, which costs $1 and provides the basic materials for three pairs, can bring in a sum of at least $5. Unique earrings of polished native stone or having some other rare appeal could be expected to sell in a souvenir store for $1.98 or more, and if you are making them in quantities, you'll find you can turn them out for about $.50 a pair. So even if you allow the shopkeeper a profit of as much as $.50 a pair for doing your selling, you clear $1 a pair. With skill and practice you'll find yourself able to make a dozen items, earrings or brooches or necklaces, all alike in less than two hours, to add up to a profit of $1 each. Not bad for something you'll love doing.

Hours

Set your own pace. You are your own factory. You can make a dozen pieces of jewelry in a week or in a day. It's best to start out initially with at least a couple of hours a day, morning, noon, or night, as you wish and the spirit moves you, until you have a little supply of merchandise that you can ask a souvenir shop, variety store, or railroad station newsstand to display and sell for you. When you see how many you can sell, then you'll know how many hours you should devote to it.

Requirements

You don't have to be an artist or have any special talent with unusual tools to create your own jewelry, but you should like creating things and be willing to experiment a little. Women, of course, are especially good at this, because they study the jewelry they see on other women and in stores and know what appeals to them and why. An interesting variation on a currently popular piece of jewelry could become a nationwide best seller. The investment is small, a few dollars at a time, and most hobby shops will be glad to show you how to make jewelry so they can convert you to a regular customer. Practice will make perfect in one of the most pleasurable jobs you could possibly find.

Future

If you like, the sky is the limit in this sideline, where one especially attractive creation could make you a fortune all by itself, if promoted nationally. But if you are not going to restrict your jewelry-making business to a local, home operation on a part-time basis, then you probably will find that some selling is involved. Instead of just contacting one friendly local souvenir shop or placing a lonesome advertisement in a popular national magazine want ad section, you'll have to get up enough nerve to seek out and collar a big department store buyer and tell him how popular your jewelry is, and how much money you both can make if his stores will sell it!

For Information

Browse through the Yellow Pages under jewelry and hobbies, and arts and crafts, for a dealer in custom jewelry kits. Or write to Don-Bar Custom Made Jewelry, 2934 W. Fullerton Ave., Chicago, Illinois 60647.

REWEAVING AND INVISIBLE MENDING

If you are handy with mending and sewing, you could become a reweaver and multiply your profits immensely while doing leisurely, light clothing repair jobs in your own time at home. Imagine, somebody burns a small hole in the arm of a suit coat or finds a jagged tear in the knee of his pants. He could throw away the suit and replace it at a cost of $50 to $100, or, chances are he'd come to you, looking for your sign, "Reweaving done here," and he'd be glad to pay $10 for that impossible mending job to look like new. You can do it through several processes today, and it is the cream of the clothing repair business—returning the biggest profits with no more work than stitching a hem, if you know how. This is an art that you'll have to learn, but if there is no local reweaver so overworked that he's glad to teach you, then you can contact the Fabricon Company and they'll set you up in business. Most people can learn to do a professional job of reweaving in a week or two of study and practice, and almost anybody can learn. There is only one tool and no materials required. This is one of those pleasurable and profitable jobs in which customers seek you out in your home and you set your own hours and your own pace in doing the work. In a couple of hours you can do two small jobs, and, at an average charge of $5 each, you will find yourself making $240 a month for two jobs a day. Or you can go at it for four hours a day or more, soliciting business from local cleaners and laundries, and multiply your profits that much more.

Earnings

They depend on the time invested, but generally figure out to about $5 an hour, which is what some professional tradesmen are paid only after years of apprenticeship.

Hours

In most situations you can set your own, working one, two, or more hours a day, morning, afternoon, or evening; but if you contract with a local cleaner to do reweaving for them, you'd better count on providing them with swift service, on a one-day basis, if possible, which means you'd probably have to work at it a little every day. Still, your nights and weekends can be your own if you wish. You're your own boss.

Requirements

If you have enough dexterity to handle a needle and thread with some efficiency, you probably qualify for learning to reweave, which is no mystery once you have the proper tool. A table or small space in a corner of a quiet room is all the space and facilities you'll need, except for the sign in the window, or, perhaps a shrewdly placed occasional newspaper want ad and telephone book listing.

Future

If you build up too much business to handle, you can easily teach someone else to do the work, or more than one person, and take in all the work available, $200 worth a week or more if you serve a chain store cleaning operation, for example. It certainly can be a full-time, full-supporting job, with the satisfaction of not only making money in a pleasant, easy task, but of saving every customer a lot of money by restoring ruined clothing to like-new condition.

For Information

Contact Fabricon Company, 1555 Howard Street, Chicago, Illinois 60626. Or write to the U.S. Department of Health, Education and Welfare for their reweaving pamphlet, Series No. 320.

MAKE RUBBER STAMPS

Want a sure-fire money-maker that requires only a relatively small investment and a little learning how? Pick up your local telephone book and flip through the Yellow Pages. Almost every listing represents a potential customer for one of the easiest selling, most useful business items that it's possible to deal in: rubber stamps. Not only that, but a third of the people listed in the white pages of your telephone book would eagerly buy their own rubber stamps to put their name and address on return envelopes or just mark them "Via Air Mail." Add it up for yourself: any single small firm in your town could use at least a half dozen rubber stamps which are recognized as big time-and-money-savers for marking mail, incoming and outgoing, order forms, checks, and even their merchandise items. Take a single rubber stamp with the words "Invoice Enclosed" or "Fragile—Handle With Care." They sell for $1 and they cost less than $.20 to make; your profit—$.80. Rubber stamps are made on a small, lever-operated machine that can produce a profit of about $20 an hour. Some beginners boast of averaging from $14 to $27 an hour their first week, working as little as an hour a day or 50 hours a week. If it sounds like a gold machine, it just might be that! Anyone who can learn to drive a car or bake an upside down cake can follow the instructions for successful operation of a small, postage-meter-size rubber stamp making machine. It is not messy work and it's not hard work; it is neat and simple. If you are a little timid about the idea of going from company to company and selling the stamps, you don't really have to do it that way. You can mail out a circular showing the full line of rubber stamps you can make, along with your prices, then just sit back and wait for the orders to come in. Of course, it's going to mean an investment of at least $.06 a mailing piece, which can run into quite a bit of money on a large scale—so be selective and be thrifty. Most rubber stamp companies offer free advertising circulars you can mail out, or you can make your own—using rubber stamps. Inquire about special business mail rates, deliver circulars yourself, or hire some other moonlighter to deliver them for you. Actually, you could afford to pay others to get orders for you and confine yourself to producing them. Besides the cost of the machine, there is a continuing small investment in materials, but, as indicated, the profit margin is wide enough to take that into consideration. They can be fun to make, too, because you create the whole product, step by step, and can test the finished work minutes later. You can stock a supply of common or standard rubber stamps such as "Fragile" in you idle hours and have a backlog on hand when the orders start coming in. There's no end to the profits you can make right in a desk-top space in the corner of a room in your house! The limits are your own time and energy; but selling is a factor, whether it's done by mail or personal contact, or just regular local advertising.

Earnings

Some indications of per hour earnings already have been given. Some machine users report weekly earnings from $100 a week part time to $250 full time. Other experienced rubber stamp makers are $20,000 a year men, but we shouldn't say men, because a lot of them are women, too.

Hours

Here is another case in which, working inside your home in your spare time, you can choose to work one hour a day or ten, one day a week or seven, and you can set your starting time for morning, noon, or night, depending on your other commitments. If you choose to sell in person, however, you'll have to set aside a few regular workday hours for that. It can be well worth it!

Requirements

There is a shoe string investment in this business, naturally— a little over $200, if you order from the factory—but there is a chance you might be able to find a used machine locally for half the price and experiment with operating it to teach yourself. Of course, the manufacturer will provide you with a complete set of instructions—not only for making rubber stamps but for marketing them. Once you commit yourself to this type of work, you may find it demanding, because people and companies ordering the stamps will expect prompt delivery, but it can be very satisfying for you to start out with a piece of raw rubber in the morning and end up in the afternoon with a check in your hands for a job well done. One caution: explore your local situation so that you are reasonable certain that the easy money aspect of this line of work hasn't already filled up your area with too many rubber stamp makers. Of course, there is always working room for another competitor, especially if you come up with a new marketing twist overlooked by the others, such as, possibly, mail-order sales in nearby areas, or even bidding on city or other large contract orders.

Future

If it is easy to make more than $200 a week full time with one small rubber stamp machine, then what's wrong with getting bigger, more efficient machines that can produce twice that profit, and hiring somebody to run them for a fraction of the value of the output? That's how small factories are started and that is precisely the future potential of this intriguing part-time or full-time occupation. Only the sales limitations place a limit on how many you can produce profitably, but if you can branch out into a broader area, through mail circulars or sending salesmen out with irresistible special prices, the business is yours and it can provide you with a life of prosperity undreamed of—until you tried it.

For Information

Write to Warner Electric Company, Inc., 1512 Jarvis Avenue, Chicago, Illinois 60626. Or contact your nearest office of the Small Business Administration, U. S. Department of Commerce, for statistics and other indications of how well such a small business venture would probably do in your specific area.

SILVER MINING AT HOME

Yes, that's right. Without really leaving your home you can cash in on today's silver boom, which precious metal speculators consider the biggest financial bonanza of the modern day. We are talking about coins—dimes, quarters, half–dollars, and silver dollars, except for the new, copper-made ones. If you think it's penny-ante, consider this: many rare coin dealers today have practically abandoned their coin collection business in favor of reaping the larger profits of sorting out silver coins for resale in quantities. This is an occupation with all the fun of a hobby, plus the thrill of discovery that can turn a small percentage profit into a real windfall. To operate your at-home silver mine, you'll need a lot of coins, which you can probably buy from banks—unrolled— or from merchants or coin machine dealers. Once you buy a quantity of coins, say $25 in dimes, you sort out all the newer, face-value copper-ringed ones and separate the valuable silver ones. Dates and letters are important on these coins, because some are worth a lot more than others. Check the classified section of the nearest big city newspaper for coin values or see a local coin dealership and ask him what coins are most in demand and what he will pay. It is not a matter of finding the occasional rare coin; that would be a high-odds treasure hunt. Just for the silver in the coins alone, dealers are paying a 10 to 20 per cent markup, and sometimes a lot more! Some dealers advertise an across-the-board offer of 16 per cent over face value for dimes and quarters by the roll. A roll of dimes ordinarily worth $10 thus becomes salable for $11.16, and if you are sorting them in quantities and constantly exchanging your money, it really adds up to big profits quickly. And it is an idle hours occupation which you can pursue while you're watching television if you wish. Sharp prospectors will invest in a coin catalog, however; they cost only a few dollars and if you discover a rare coin among those you are sorting, the one dime will repay your investment and add a handsome profit. Imagine! If you think you are flat broke right this minute, except for a handful of change in your pocket or in a sugar jar, what if there were a certain Lincoln penny among your coins worth more than $100? There are a lot of them and they are scattered all over the country in circulation.

Earnings

A $10 roll of fairly common 1954 quarters can sell for $18 or $20; plain 1942 pennies in a $.50 roll sell for more than $5; a $10 roll of 1965 half-dollars can sell for about $15. Silver dollars sell for $1.65 to $1.95 each, regardless of how old they are. And there is always the excitement of finding a rare old nickel, dime, quarter, or even penny that is worth a hundred times its face value to collectors! Some very big investors are buying silver coins and putting them in bank vaults by the bagful, anticipating another silver price rise which will make them rich. Depending on how much time you invest in sorting out coins, you could cash in on the bonanza to the extent of $20 a week on a strictly part-time basis; it is practically a guaranteed income.

Hours

You'll have to devote at least two hours a day to silver hunting to make it profitable, but you can pick the time of day when you feel like doing it, and you could be baby-sitting or watching television or sharing a cup of coffee with a neighbor while you are doing it.

Requirements

No special skill is required, but a small investment is necessary to start you off with your first $25 worth of coins to sift, plus the cost of a coin collector's bible, which is well worth the initial cost. A sharp eye for small dates and letters, the most significant marks on coins, can make your fortune. There is no actual selling involved in this part-time occupation, because the buyers are eager to pay the going profit or more. But you should have enough nerve to go and ask at an amusement park, busy department store, bank, or coin machine distributorship for the opportunity to sort out their coins. Chances are, if you are well known in town and offer to count their daily receipts for them, they'll be glad to let you have access to their money without buying it. If it is necessary that you take the money to your home for counting before depositing it in the bank for them, you probably would be required to be insured against possible loss or thefts, which a bonding company can do for a small fee.

Future

This is a business that has attracted some of the shrewdest financial minds of the current day. Buyers who are willing to pay up to $1.50 or more on the dollar for quantities of silver coins are banking on the fact that silver will nearly double in value in the next few years. They figure if they can store away tens of thousands of dollars in silver coins now, at almost any price, they will double their money in a matter of only a few years.

For Information

Contact a local coin dealer or read the want ads from a big city newspaper under coins. Books on coin values also will be available at any bookstore. Or write Jonathan Coins, 535 West Manchester Boulevard, Inglewood, California.

WIN A PRIZE!

Oh, sure, you may say, I never have any luck. Well, when you see a picture of a woman boarding a plane who has just won a round-the-world trip, chances are she is one of the many prize-winners who work at it professionally. And most of the time the merchandise prize can be exchanged for cash. There are several companies, nationwide, which keep track of all the big contests going on and for a small fee they send out regular, up-to-date mailings about them, including, in the case of puzzles and other competitions—the answers! It is completely legal and a lot of people are trying their hand at it in their spare time. After all, what could be more fun than a puzzle or contest? And when you are shooting at a possible $10,000 prize or a new car, the thrill of it can be helpful if you are imaginative enough to write in 25 possibly hitting the jackpot is exciting. Most of the contests take no special skill, but do require a boxtop or facsimile to enter. And words or less, something like "Why I prefer Snow soap above all others. . . ."

Earnings

You have to face the prospect at the outset that this is strictly a long shot proposition with no guarantee that you ever will win any more than the small prizes some contests give out just for entering, because there are thousands of persons entering every contest. On the other hand, if you enter every imaginable contest, the odds in your favor increase that much, and let's face it: sombody's got to win, so why shouldn't it be you?

Hours

Since it is hard to draw the line between where the fun and where the work in this pursuit leave off, you can call it a hobby and try your hand at it for an hour a day or less, at your own convenience. Just don't miss a single one.

Requirements

All you need is a little enthusiasm for the prospect of toying with puzzles and words, and who doesn't like this kind of fun? They even do it at parties! You'll have to invest a few dollars in one of the "insider" magazines that tell you all about all the current contests, and postage will cost you a few cents per entry. You don't have to buy the products a contest will suggest for their boxtops and labels; according to law, no contest can require a purchase, so all you have to do is draw up a copy of the label or boxtop and send that in.

Future

This will never be more than a part-time pursuit, and probably should be done in connection with some other moonlighting occupation. But if you hit the jackpot, it can change your whole life—a new home, a new car, travel, and money in the bank!

For Information

Write to The Prizewinner, Robert Spence Publications, Inc., 1315 Central Avenue, St. Petersburg, Florida 33733; or Puzzle Lovers Club, Box 2, Prince Street Station, New York, New York 10012.

BE A RESEARCH PANELIST

Do you know that there are companies which will pay you for telling them your honest opinion of their products? It is part of market research, one of the biggest businesses in America today. For example, a soap company invents a new washing powder. If they can get the opinion of one thousand average housewives from all over America about how attractive their package is and how good their soap is, it serves as a guideline which tells them whether they should invest millions of dollars in mass production and advertising in order to sell the product nationwide to millions of housewives. To them, it is a legitimate business expense. They pay you and expect an honest opinion, that's all.

Earnings

Don't count on a steady income from opinion research unless you go at it in a big way and have your whole women's club or neighborhood sampling products. A $5 or $10 fee per product is common, and you get to keep the product, of course. Sometimes as much as $100 is paid, but these testing jobs are irregular and you'll be lucky to get more than one a month, so it is best to combine this moonlighting job with other occupations.

Hours

You set your own. It is very flexible and most jobs, from the opening of the package to the return mailing of your opinion, will be only an hour at your own convenience.

Requirements

No special marketing knowledge or writing skill is needed. The companies are paying for your personal opinion in your own words, nothing more. You'll need the initiative to look up, in magazines, big city telephone books, or library reference books, the names of big firms or their market research companies. Write letters to the companies or market research firms and tell them you are willing to serve as an opinion panelist for product testing. They will want full data on your age, income, and education.

Future

There is a possibility of expanding such an endeavor in ways that will pay off with big money. Suppose you round up one hundred women in your town who will fill in questionnaires on products, with their opinions? You have organized the basis for a local poll which could consider popular questions of today for radio and television programs or for individual politicians or for product merchandisers. They'll pay for such a service, and pay well. Or, if you could select and sift out a thousand names around the country, in all major cities and small towns, people whom you could count on for a reply by mail, you would have a service that would be very valuable in political circles and for marketing experts. There would be a lot of unrewarded groundwork, but once such an organization was set up, you've got your own business, and it can be big! Ever heard of the Gallup Poll or the TV Rating System? They make millions for opinions.

For Information

It is best to stick to your own individual inquiries to companies and market research firms you find in the suggested lists. One firm which promises to get you opinion work, but charges a $10 registration and processing fee, is World Field Research, Main Street, Mineola, New York 11501. Another which will train you for professional interviewing offers a free booklet: Universal Schools, Department 5404, 6801 Hillcrest, Dallas, Texas 75205.

RAISE SMALL ANIMALS

If you love living things, here's the moonlighting job for you, one that calls for no special skills other than tender care and regular attention. Most important is a place to keep the animals and a foreknowledge of where to sell them. Some people make a good, steady income by raising in their own back yard an abundance of little creatures like mice, guinea pigs, rabbits, chinchillas, or even frogs, worms, minnows, and spiders! The advantages of earning money this way are clear. First, almost anybody can do it; second, you don't have to leave your own home; third, most of the work can be done in less than an hour a day; and last but not least, the cute little things can be fun. Here are details about the most popular species.

Chinchillas—with their beige, white, or silver furs making them the richest of all small animals to raise, can produce unlimited income from a reasonably small investment to start. A chinchilla coat may sell for as high as $100,000. The animals are reported to be reasonably clean, ordorless, and noiseless, and can be raised in your garage. You'll have to invest in an initial set of one male and three or four females, considered the best production ratio, and, of course, cages. Feeding and cleaning takes only a few minutes a day, on a regular schedule, and their food is inexpensive. Before investing, make sure that you have in writing a pledge for

help in marketing the full-grown animals, if not an outright promise to buy. Many organizations will supply chinchillas to you,
teach you how to raise them, and market them. For information,
contact the nearest chinchilla ranch listed in your local telephone
book Yellow Pages or write: Nationwide Chinchillas, 14001 Ventura Boulevard, Sherman Oaks, California; or Mutation Chinchilla
Company, 4654 Lankershim Boulevard, North Hollywood, California. Expect to pay a minimum of $100 a pair.

Rabbits—there are at least three ways to make money raising
rabbits, and these engaging animals are famous for their swift
multiplication. Angora rabbits grow a coat of wool that is sheared
and woven just like wool, but is soft as a feather, and much in
demand for gloves and clothing linings. There are funny, long-
eared rabbits that sell like hot cakes at Easter time, but this is
strictly a once-a-year market. And rabbits also are a delicacy for
food. The initial investment is small. Best to start with at least
two pairs and plenty of cage space. Almost without exception, the
best place to start a rabbit raising business is at your nearest
local pet shop. The owner will be glad to advise you on the care
and feeding of the animals, but the most important thing to ask
is this: will he buy them back from you, or can he tell you where
to sell them? Don't plan on rabbits if you are confined to garage
space. You'll need a far corner of the back yard for these bundles
of fur.

Guinea Pigs—also called cavies, are smaller and can be raised
in smaller areas for sale as pets or to pet stores and science laboratories. You can start with a ratio of one male to a half dozen fe-
males. Sell them yourself by placing an ad in the pets for sale
column of your local newspaper, or ask at a nearby college where
they procure their guinea pigs for science classes. They will tell
you the name of a broker or large laboratory where you can
inquire about mass sales of all your guinea pig offspring.

Frogs—rural areas are best for raising these profitable creatures. Millions of frogs are in demand at the best restaurants
across the country, where their legs are a high-priced delicacy.
Laboratories and schools also require a large number. If there's
a small pond in your area on the property of a neighbor who'll let
you stock it with tadpoles or full-grown frogs, you can go about
this business in a big way; they'll multiply by the thousands.
Or you can create your own fenced-in pool, 25 feet by 25 feet, and
you'll soon be dealing in them by the hundreds. They don't have

to be fed, but find a distant spot for them because they can get noisy. Ask the manager of a local restaurant who supplies him with frogs and contact that person to see if he'll buy frogs directly from you.

Earthworms and Minnows—if you live in an area where fishing is popular, chances are you could start a profitable sideline by raising worms or minnows for bait. Bait wholesalers, found in the Yellow Pages or by asking at a sporting goods store, can supply you with breeding stock. They lay eggs which produce mature worms in three months; thousands of them can be raised in a box 2 feet square filled with loam. They sell for about a dime a dozen, but if you post a sign at busy fishing spots and at sporting goods stores, you'll be dealing in dollars in no time. Similarly, minnows can be raised in small tanks in your back yard. They multiply swiftly and are considered a prime bait by fishermen, so you'll have no trouble selling them.

Spiders were mentioned above, and seriously, they can be profitable. Their fine web has been used for gun sights and other industrial purposes. But this is a special project, and unless you're willing to spend some time learning the tricks of the trade, better stick to the more common of creatures. On the other hand, if a demand exists in your area for some unusual creature, be it spider, snake, or snail, you could corner the market all by yourself.

Earnings

What you make from raising small animals will depend on whether you choose the humble, penny worm or the rich chinchilla, of course. It will also hinge on how many you set out to produce. Sales will be seasonal and irregular and can run from a few dollars a day to thousands a year. It's up to you.

Hours

In almost every case, the care and feeding of small animals is something you can do in a few minutes a day, every day, and you can choose the time of the chore to suit your convenience; morning, noon, or night.

Requirements

Little or no skill is involved, but you have to care and you should'nt be scared of tiny animals. An initial investment in breeding stock also will be needed and these prices must be obtained locally. Also, you need suitable space and such accommodations as cages and food. You have to market your animals, but in most cases you should arrange their sale in advance, so that the product is actually pre-sold.

Future

The sky is the limit in most cases of raising small animals. A big frog farm operation can net $50,000 a year and a few dozen chinchillas can even top that. Once you know your animals and know the market, you can take steps to expand into the big money.

For Information

Besides specific Yellow Pages breeding contacts and pet stores, contact the nearest office of the U. S. Department of Agriculture for handy booklets and instructions on the care, feeding, and marketing of specific small animals. Also, before you start out, check with your city or county Department of Zoning Regulation and Department of Health, to make sure there are no restrictions on raising small animals in your neighborhood.

BE A NOTARY PUBLIC

Here is a constant money-making service that you can provide right in your front room, without ever going out. People come to you. When they need legal documents witnessed, they'll drive all over town looking for that familiar sign, and if it's posted outside your house, they'll stop. It only takes a minute to watch the customer sign and then stamp your official seal on the document, collecting a dollar. It doesn't take too many customers a week to make it a profitable sideline. A notary public is a respected, permanent citizen in his town. You don't have to understand complicated legal documents. All you are verifying with your signature is that it was signed in your presence. No selling is involved, since people come to you, but it may build business to place an occasional two-line ad in your local newspaper to familiarize people with your name so they will bring their documents to you. And it also might be a good idea to pass around business cards—especially to real estate agents and similar firms that deal in large numbers of such papers. List in the Yellow Pages too.

Earnings

You can charge a dollar for every paper you notarize, or even more if you provide a special service such as having blank legal forms handy or agreeing to notarize a document at a late hour or in somebody else's home. The fee is small, but if you have many people coming to you—and they say paper work makes the world go around today—the income can add up considerably. And this standby income is for life! You keep renewing your license period-ically.

Hours

The hours run from sunrise to midnight when someone is likely to stop for notarizing, and even though you don't have to stay at home every minute of every day, it's best that you're available most of the time. So as not to disappoint too many customers, when you're out try a little door clock that says, "The notary will be back at _____ ." Maybe they'll wait or come back.

Requirements

All you need to be a notary public is to be a citizen and to be age 21 or over. You will have to fill out an application with your state government and pay a fee, which usually is $5. In some states you must post a bond, but a bonding company will supply this at a surprisingly low cost—less than $3 for a $1,000 bond.

Future

There's really no full-time income opportunity in being a notary other than the benefit of a lifetime extra income. You can branch out into preparing and selling pads of legal forms connected with your sideline, once you become familiar with the work, and this could expand your basic irregular income.

For Information

Contact the office of the Secretary of State in the nearest large city or the state capital, and ask them about an application for a notary public appointment. They will send you the papers. There is a company which specializes in assisting you to become a notary public. They provide you with full, step-by-step instructions and legal forms for an initial $12.50 fee, guaranteeing that you will get the appointment or your money back. Contact: Stationers Exchange, 405 Richardt Avenue, Evansville, Illinois 47711.

CASH FROM CONCRETE

Even without special skills or training, if you can follow a set of instructions as simple as putting together a baby's tricycle, then you can turn a sack of plain, ordinary concrete into $200, and people will start calling you an artist as well! You can cast concrete—a simple mixture of cement, sand, and water—into dozens of shapes, making birdbaths, benches, fountains, wishing wells, patio chairs and tables, planters, stepping stones, and even animals. Any building supply store will tell you how. You simply mix the concrete at a leisurely pace in your own back yard, pour it into molds, and wait for it to dry. In a few days spare-time work you can literally fill your front yard with these traffic-stopping works of concrete art. Watch the neighbors and passersby stop and ask how much. You can sell them astonishingly inexpensively and still clear 500 per cent profit for your labors. Or you can ask a local garden and patio furniture dealer if he'd like to buy quantities of your articles for resale. You'll not only reap a big profit from selling these items, but you'll have the satisfaction of outdoor, creative work that places objects of beauty all over town. Of course, birdbaths and garden seats are seasonal items, but you can round out your year and secure a regular income by creating other handy objects such as building blocks and indoor pottery items. In winter you can work in a garage or basement.

Earnings

On the average, you can count on a minimum of $5 an hour for your efforts, with a very small investment. Cement costs $1 to $2 a sack; white sand runs about $2.95 a yard; and the amount of water is inconsequential. The return, depending on the article made, will be fifteen to twenty times the cost of the materials. Visit shops selling such items and see what they charge. Chop off 25 per cent to attract bargain hunters, and you'll still be making plenty.

Hours

You can vary the hours to suit yourself, but in a chilly spring, for example, count on working during sunlight hours—or indoors. From one hour a day to forty a week can be invested in this job. Weekends are ideal for the part-time worker. A lot of time will be spent just waiting for the ingredients to dry.

Requirements

No special talents or skill are necessary, especially if you're willing to invest in buying the original molds to start with. You should like working in the sun and creating things, and be able to follow a simple set of instructions. The only material requirements to set up a complete home concrete products plant for any number of designs are a shaping box, a finishing wheel, and a smoothing guide, all of which can be hand made from common materials available in your own town for about $5. Several companies, for relatively small fees ranging from $10 to $15, are eager to start you out in this enjoyable, profitable business with a complete set of instructions and their own patented processes for creating unbelievably beautiful concrete objects of art that sell on sight. You don't have to sell these objects. Ask a building supply or garden-patio shop manager and he'll be glad to buy all you can make of certain items. Or just let them sit in your front yard and wait for the customers to come to you. Of course, a little advertising will mean more money in your pocket.

Future

Concrete products can turn into a full-time manufacturing job for you if you work at it. As you go from one mold to another you are adding to the size of your business, and if your product is priced right and selling fast, you'd better do some figuring. It may pay you to quit your job and become a full-time concrete products manufacturer. See Chapter 8 for details. It's usually seasonal in nature, but some concrete products makers earn enough in the spring and summer to take it easy and not work at all in the winter!

For Information

Write Hollywood Cement Craft, 602 East Athens Street, Altadena, California 91001; National Potteries Company, 1126 Third Avenue East, Grand Rapids, Minnesota; or Dewson Carlayne Castings, 1803 Fremont Street, Rapid City, South Dakota 57701.

CLIPPING BUREAU

If you love to read, you can start a small, leisurely, at-home clipping service which will pay you big dividends. A clipping bureau works on this basic idea: a company or a public figure from out of town may miss a write up in your local newspaper. They'll be glad to pay a dollar for it, perhaps more, and just for the one story or the page—not the whole newspaper. Now, some clipping services operate on a national or international scale, subscribing to practically every major newspaper and magazine printed; but the moonlighter can start on a much smaller scale at home, with a minimum investment. Suppose you live in Boston. You should subscribe to all newspapers in the area, and later can expand into the big cities of Maine, New Hampshire, Vermont, Connecticut, and Rhode Island. Buy a supply of postal cards and order a rubber stamp that reads something like, "A story about you or your company appeared in the local newspaper on such and such a date. Send $1 and a copy will be mailed to you." Of course, you leave blanks for the party's name, newspaper name, and date. Most people eagerly respond. In the case of most public figures and big companies, you won't need any more detailed address than is mentioned in the story. A couple of hints: clip only locally originating stories and columns, because syndicated columns and wire service stories, identified by the initials AP, UPI, Reuters, or other syndication credit lines in small type, appear all over the country. It is the local stories that out-of-town people find hard to get. Second, when sending out cards to companies, address them to the attention of the Public Relations Director; he will be the man most eager to get a copy. Another way to start an at-home clipping bureau is to contact public relations and advertising companies in the nearest large city and ask them if they would be willing to pay for regular clippings about their clients from a certain list of newspapers. Such firms can prove their worth to clients with such clippings, so they are eager for them. As a matter of fact, if there are other papers they would like watched for clippings, chances are they will be glad to pay for the subscriptions themselves. And there you are; you've already expanded. There are money-making sidelines, too. You can clip industrial stories and send them to trade magazines, or you can compile lists of brides-to-be or births for companies, described elsewhere, which pay for these names.

Earnings

They will vary and will be irregular. One day a single newspaper may yield a dozen items worth clipping and mailing a notice card, and if six responses come back, you've made a $5.90 profit on a $.10 newspaper. People love to see their names in print, so the return is usually high. If you find you're not getting the proper response, maybe you need a little help and should try the information contact below. Even on a small scale you should make approximately $150 a month for your service.

Hours

When the mail arrives, you can start, and if you have half a dozen papers to go through, you should be able to clip them at a leisurely pace over a cup of coffee in little more than an hour. The time of day is flexible, of course; you could do your clipping at night, but then you'd probably lose a day's delay in mailing out your notices. If you have a dozen papers, figure on two hours. The time of day is not too important; you can choose your own hours. One thing is important: the job must be done regularly, daily. Once you get behind it's hard to catch up.

Requirements

If you like to read, you've got it made, and you'll really find yourself building up a broad storehouse of information. The newspapers (you can subscribe by the month) will be your major initial investment, probably $25 a month, and postal cards (one hundred for $6) but if they bring you back $50, the investment is small—actually about $13 a week for $50 a week, your pay for as little as seven hours work. It figures out to more than $5 an hour for enjoyable, easy work. You'll have to learn how to file the clips until the orders come in, and, starting out, you'd better keep track of costs and income, so you can see if you're making all the profit you can.

The Future

Expansion, and increased investment, could turn a small, part-time clipping bureau into a fully staffed, eight-hour a day operation. If you had just a few big clients, and newspapers coming from cities all over the country, you'd be up to your ears in clippings—and dollars. Some celebrities and politicians pay out thousands a year for this service. Keeping track of their fame, their public image, is the most valuable service they can buy.

For Information

Check your local or nearest big city Yellow Pages for public relations firms and advertising agencies. Or, for a fully detailed list of instructions and possible customers, contact American Industries, Post Office Box 56, Muncie, Kansas; or Walter, Post Office Box 1360, Erie, Pennsylvania.

LISTS AND IDEAS FOR SALE

Talking about profits from newspapers, there is money to be made by compiling from your local newspapers lists of brides-to-be, new graduates, new mothers, new residents, new homeowners and the like. If you are going through the newspapers anyway, it's not hard to get in the habit of building up such lists. It doesn't take much time and it can form a regular small addition to your income. Call or write the nearest mail-order firms and ask them what they need and what they'll pay. You can also keep your eyes open for interesting little local stories in particular fields of business and industry. Small business, association, and trade magazines you've probably never heard of circulate throughout the country and some of them long for local items they can rewrite or include in their columns.

Earnings

For name lists, it's a matter of pennies per name; but, particularly if you are clipping other items, the pennies can add up. Clippings you send to trade magazines, depending on their importance, can be worth $1 to $5 each.

Hours

Flexible but daily, a minimum of an hour per day.

Requirements

You should have access to at least half a dozen newspapers daily to make these pursuits profitable. But here's a good tip: they can be yesterday's papers free from a friend or neighbor. Curiosity is a big asset. Invest $6 in a copy of the current year's Writer's Market for a complete list of trade magazines and descriptions of their needs and payments. Get a rubber stamp with a name of your clipping service so that you can send a letterhead type bill along with clippings you mail to likely prospects. You shouldn't be an easily frustrated type in this business. Some magazines won't respond at all; others will dash off an immediate check for $1 or $5 or more. It's simply trial and error. It's the only kind of selling involved in this quiet, easy, at-home job.

Future

Name lists can be built up on a national level by swapping around and broadening your research, and this is one possibility of expansion worth exploring for bigger profits. The trade magazine clippings are more promising careerwise. Look up the trade magazine you are sending a clipping to. If the Writer's Market indicates they pay worthwhile amounts, and some do pay $50 or $100 and more for stories, send along a note with the clipping, asking if they'd like a more detailed story. If they do, telephone the company involved and ask them for full information. They'll be glad to supply it to you; it's free publicity for them. Send it off to the magazine. You've just become a free-lance writer!

For Information

Try the Yellow Pages for mail-order firms that might be interested in specific name lists. You may have to go to the directory of the largest city in your area. For trade magazine clipping, the best available information and addresses are available in the Writer's Market, at a bookstore or library. Or write to Walter, Post Office Box 1360, Erie, Pennsylvania, for information on their list of publications and their needs.

BECOME AN UPHOLSTERER

This is a trade you will have to study and learn, either by working for an experienced upholsterer or by taking a course; there is no other way. But the rewards in lifetime steady income, the fun of creative work, and the possibility of your own full-time business if you wish to expand from a part-time job, make it one of the most lucrative and appealing jobs today. Chances are that you are sitting in an upholstered chair this very minute. It could have cost from $50 to $200; if it's a sofa, from $100 to $1,000. If it has become worn or outdated, wouldn't the owner rather pay a good fee to have it restored instead of replacing it for a much greater cost? This is the opportunity for an experienced upholsterer, and there is business galore everywhere. Sometimes one little $1.50 newspaper ad will bring in a month's work. You can operate from your own home, basement, or garage, on a part-time basis, or save on transporting the furniture by working in the customer's home.

Earnings

The potential income from upholstering is limited only by your own energy. Charges for the labor of reupholstering a quality chair run about $50, in addition to the profit a tradesman makes on the fabric chosen for recovering. For a sofa the price and the amount of material used is about double. So there can be an income of $75 to $150 and more on each job.

Hours

Few jobs will take less than half a day, but if you are working in your home, you don't have to finish a piece of upholstery all at once. You can set your hours, working two hours one night and two the next, for instance, or working weekends—any hours convenient to you. If you want to make a good side income and keep your customers pleased with your service, better arrange to work at least eight hours a week at it. Or you can approach it more leisurely; buy run-down sofas and chairs for $10 or $15 "junk" prices, take your time restoring them, and then sell them for a huge profit as like-new furniture.

Requirements

Training will be necessary, of course. The work is not difficult, but there are many tricks to the trade. A few tools and access to materials, plus a willingness to work are all that you need to start on this interesting career. Think of what you can do to your own furniture, for a starter; for a little material and a little time gaining experience, you can have the best upholstered furniture in town. Both men and women do this work.

Future

Your own business on a full-time basis, perhaps employing others to do the actual work, can result from diligent pursuit of this occupation—if you can find a regular route of work or attract enough jobs by the reputation of doing good work. Often upholstery cleaning as a full-time business is combined with rug and drapery cleaning or upholstery recovering operations.

For Information

Contact the Modern Upholstery Institute, Post Office Box 899, Orange, California. Or look up upholsterers in your Yellow Pages; call them and ask if they would train you on a part-time basis.

SEWING

If you are handy with a needle and thread, or can learn to be with just a little practice, this can provide a regular small income for you without even getting out of a rocking chair. You will be surprised at how many top rated dress shops do not do their own alterations, and, in these days of fluctuating hemlines, every season women take their clothes out of the closet and find they need alteration to be in style. So there is plenty of work, even if you specialize in nothing more complicated than hemlines. Give your name, address, and telephone number to dress shops where they do not alter and to cleaning shops in the same situation. You don't need a sewing machine, of course, although this could make some jobs easier. You will need a variety of thread colors and needles. If you are an expert with sewing (some relative or adult education class can teach you to be one), you can offer to do more complex alterations to custom fit garments, or make whole dresses from patterns and yardage goods. Remember, a lot of people sew for the sheer enjoyment of it. Put a sign in your window, "Hemlines Fixed—Alterations," an ad in your local want ad section, and a listing in the telephone book, and you're in business.

Earnings

The pay is not exorbitant, but the work is not hard, either. A $2 charge for raising or lowering a hemline is small enough to bring customers back again and again, and you could do half a dozen a day by hand, more than fifty a week if you attracted enough business.

Hours

Flexible. You will be able to select your own time of day and the number of hours will depend on how much business you bring in. A few hours a day, or evening, will make for a nice, steady, part-time income.

Requirements

You must be able to sew, of course, at least to the extent of hem-lines, and you should be willing to learn more about the art as you go along. A sign in your window won't bring the customers running right away, so you've got to be enterprising enough to visit a few dress shops and ask for their business, or to place a newspaper ad. Sewing is an enjoyable pastime, but it requires neatness and care. Remember, you'll be handling other people's valuable garments. Treat them with respect. Set aside a corner table for your goods and your work.

Future

If you can learn dressmaking you can earn high pay creating beautiful gowns for proms, weddings, and parties, and if your work is good, word will get around. You could find yourself with a full-time job or even a dressmaking shop on your hands—all from a small start with needle and thread and the eagerness to learn!

For Information

Contact the nearest home economics education teacher, high school or college, or inquire at church about sewing clubs. Sewing machine sales outlets teach machine operation free to induce you to buy their machines. For customers, if you already know sewing well enough, visit dress shops where they do not advertise "free alterations" and cleaning stores, where people often ask about re-pairing hem tears or altering their garments. Beware of distant companies which advertise for you to buy their pre-cut products for you to stitch at home, unless you don't mind the fact that you'll probably have to go out and sell them yourself to earn your money back. In some cases, however, such firms state unconditionally in writing that they will buy back the completed articles from you at a profit.

MAKE CUSTOM DRAPERIES

Here is a distinguished, profitable job in the interior decorating line that doesn't require extensive schooling or a definite artistic inclination, but can be almost as profitable and every bit as satis-fying personally. Most of the trick of drapery-making is measuring and cutting, since they have ingenious little devices for setting and fixing the pleats. Every time somebody moves into a new house or apartment, and hundreds of people move every day, you have a prospect for draperies. You go to their homes for measurements and to show them sample materials, and you notify them when their drapes are ready. It's a cash business so you are immediately reimbursed for your materials and paid well for your work. It is bright, cheerful work. You are invited into the best of homes and participate in decorating them. There can be profitable sidelines, such as providing matching bedspreads, slipcovers and the like, and if you gain the proper experience, you can even offer window styling advice, pointing out the several possible variations for hanging draperies.

Earnings

Some people who make draperies in their own home report making up to $100 a day, exclusive of their material costs; but you can work on a much smaller scale, doing one job a week for the same sum. Your business will be better, however, if you take two smaller jobs and deliver each within a few days, because when people want draperies, they usually want them quickly to dress up a new household.

Hours

You can set your own hours, but in drapery-making, you had better be able to devote at least three or four hours a day to the work in order to get it done quickly.

Requirements

You will need some training unless you are one of those sewing geniuses who can take apart their own draperies and see what the trick is in gathering the pleats, and what the real width is to various proportions of window. You'll have to advertise a little, in the newspaper want ads, on supermarket and apartment building bulletin boards, and in some key spots like model homes in new subdivisions. You will also need a few basic tools and a good long table, occupying perhaps half of a spare room, clean basement, or garage. And you will need a sample kit of materials. Yardage goods makers probably will be glad to provide free samples of their current merchandise in the hopes you'll be buying quantities from them. They'll also give you the per yard cost. Professional drapery makers charge as much as $12 per width of drapery, and receive up to double the price they invest in the fabric, so you'll have to be able to shop around in your area and determine what prices are being asked. Make yours a tempting bit lower. You will do most of the work in the comfort of your home, but you must be able to get out of the house, to meet customers and help them select fabrics, to measure windows and procure your yardage goods. If you're good with talking to people you may be able to arrange to pay for yard goods after you've collected for the completed draperies.

Future

Without doubt drapery-making could develop into a full-time job and even a fully staffed store operation bringing in hundreds of dollars in income each week and stocking its own materials to profit by their sale. Sidelines like drapery sliding rods, installation, curtains, and even complete interior decoration are possible. The sky is the limit if you can learn and have the ambition to keep working at a good thing. Some husband-wife teams enjoy this work together.

For Information

Consult your Yellow Pages under draperies, yardage goods, and interior decorating to see if there is a likely outlet that would teach you basic drapery-making. Or for a full course by mail, covering every detail, supplying all tools, and even offering wholesale fabrics, write Custom Drapery Institute, Box 555, Orange, California 92669.

TELEPHONE ANSWERING

Answering the telephone for other people, in your own home, can bring in a steady side income with only a small effort if you're going to be home anyway; or, if you really want to work at it, it can develop into a full-time business of your own.

Earnings

Telephone answering service rates, depending on the competition, the number of calls received, and the hours you make your phone available, range from a minimum of $5 to $25 per customer per month, plus, of course, any toll charges you accept.

Hours

For most customers you will be required to be there to answer the telephone at least from 9:00 A.M., to 5:00 P.M., and for others, until midnight.

Requirements

If you can answer the telephone by it's number, write down the name of the calling party, his telephone number, and the name of the person to whom he wishes to speak, all you have to do is relay this information to the party when he or she calls in later. A little desk space near the telephone is required, and a private line will be mandatory if you have more than an average number of calls coming in. You'll have to advertise your service in the local newspapers.

Future

A full-time telephone answering service can be big business, with more than one telephone and more than one answerer involved. It only takes about a dozen customers to make the service an income of a couple of hundred dollars a month, so if there are forty-eight or one hundred forty-eight customers, the income skyrockets.

For Information

Check with the answering services in your own town and nearby towns and ask their rates and services for a comparison, or question somebody you know who uses one. Most salesmen, small businesses, and self-employed persons do.

TELEPHONE SOLICITING OR SURVEYS

Another comfortable job that can be done right at home if you like to talk to people. Many sales organizations and other companies use this method for contacting potential customers. They assign you a section of the telephone book or a list to call, and a printed copy of what you are to say, along with the answers to typical questions. You go down the list, calling each number and saying whatever you have to say.

Earnings

Many firms will guarantee $2 an hour, or the equivalent pay on a per call basis, but the real income benefits of this job come in that one out of ten or twenty calls when a prospect is interested in a product and agrees to see a salesman; if a sale is made, the solicitor usually gets a commission.

Hours

Usually two or more weekday hours, between 10:00 A. M. and 8:00 P.M., are required on this job; the more regular the hours, the more steady the pay.

Requirements

As long as you are not afraid to talk to strangers as a representative of the firm you are working for, and have a telephone in your home and a little quiet time, you've got what it takes for this job.

Future

Many soliciting jobs are temporary in nature; but if you become known for doing this job well, companies will soon be contacting you and you'll end up with all the work you can handle, and the resulting high income. Poll-taking and surveys could be developed as part of your work, too.

For Information

Contact firms who advertise for solicitors, not only in your local paper but in nearby large cities, telephone insurance companies, book sales firms, or any large organization with a product to sell, and ask to speak to the sales manager. For poll-taking or surveys, call or write to pollsters in major cities in your area or in New York. Or write Universal, 6801 Hillcrest, Dallas, Texas 75205, for free booklet on survey taking.

Chapter 3
WORKING FOR OTHERS

The quickest, easiest way to earn extra dollars is to find somebody who will pay you to work for them a few hours or more in the evenings, after your regular job, or on weekends. You seek an employer who is willing to hire you for whatever hours you are available, and you both benefit. Probably he does not have enough work to require putting somebody on the job for a full eight-hour shift, and if this is the case, he saves by your willingness to work part time; or if he has plenty of work to be done, or hours to be filled, there may be a shortage of workers to do it and the employer is able to fill one full-time shift by hiring two persons for half shifts. Often employers, especially in work such as stores and restaurants, where there are regular rush hour periods, are eager to hire people to supplement their regular staff during the busy time. Again, they save and you profit.

The most clear-cut advantage of working for someone else is that you are paid regularly, an agreed sum per hour or week, so you know from the first day just how much extra income you will be making; you can count on it. Also, the job usually does not make an excessive demand on you as far as responsibility is concerned, so you are not drained physically and mentally by putting in a longer work day or week. The boss has all the business worries. You just do your job, whatever is required, and go home and forget it.

There are two considerations in choosing such a second job, and they can be important. Do you seek work that is the same as your regular job or something different? The advantage of selecting similar work to your regular employment lies in the fact that you can probably command a better wage on the basis of your experience. But if you are not particularly enthusiastic about your full-time work, why pursue it in moonlighting, too? The chances are the extra hours doing the same kind of work will seem harder to you, like putting in several hours of overtime every day or an extra day a week.

It may be better to secure a job that is different from what you do regularly. Then the extra hours will be relieved not only by a change of scene but by a whole new occupation.

On the other hand, your first avenue of approach in finding a moonlighting job may be your current boss. A straightforward approach such as: "I need more money, and I know I'm not in line for a raise just now, but I'd be willing to work Saturdays or Sundays or overtime in the evening," might solve your problem right there. For the same reasons that any employer finds it better to hire part-time help in some cases, your boss may be willing to increase your working hours enough to give you that extra income you need.

Sometimes, however, seniority, union rules, civil service regulations, store and factory hours, or other circumstances rule out the possibility of your working extra hours on your full-time job. Those who must look elsewhere will find numerous job ideas in this chapter. Remember this: they are only ideas, suggestions.

Your best asset in locating a part-time job is imagination. Assuming that you've already read the want ad sections of your local newspapers and found nothing that appeals to you, don't crumple up the newspaper and throw it away—not yet. Aside from your own personal knowledge of your neighborhood and what is going on in your city, your local newspaper is still the best guide to what's happening. And if you're startled by the lack of part-time job offerings in the want ads, the fact is that part-time jobs are seldom advertised. Most big employers tend to think in terms of full-time shifts and smaller operators may be trying to save the part-time job opening for their brother-in-law or some friend, or they may just realize that part-time jobs of this kind are so much in demand they will have no trouble finding an applicant. But the jobs exist.

First of all, what about the employers who are trying to hire full-time help? You have the clear indication that they need help, for one thing. Maybe they never thought of a part-time employee. So why not apply and tell them you are available part time if they would consider hiring you on that basis? It doesn't hurt to ask.

While you've still got your newspaper out, look at the big display ads in all sections. What are the busiest stores? Which are the most crowded restaurants? Where are the crowds going? Who is running a big sale? What are the big selling seasonal items and what businesses are they associated with? Scan the news columns, too. Is the airport jammed with nightly or weekend crowds? Is the post office overloaded with work? Is there a convention coming to town? Is the bank expanding? Are they building a new hotel or apartment building? Are J.C. Smith and son of Smith and Son Hardware going on an extended European vacation? Who's going to mind the store?

If you adjust your thinking to the job you want, and keep your eyes open for what's happening in your city and nearby, you'll find it. To suggest a few possibilities which you may have overlooked, we offer the following part-time jobs list reminding you again that they are only a sampling of all the many opportunities that may exist for you:

MILKMAN

Many people are jogging around town for exercise today, but you can get yours before the regular workday starts by delivering milk for a local dairy on a regular early morning route. It's outdoor work and you've earned your extra pay before you even start your regular day.

Earnings

Over $3 an hour and it can be a lot more if the dairy gives a bonus for extra customers you bring in.

Hours

Pre-dawn. Three, four, or five hours between midnight and 6:00 A.M., usually. Sometimes later. Sometimes a full, eight-hour job.

Requirements

A driver's license, general good health, and dependability.

Future

You can build a part-time route into a big, full-time route or become foreman or dispatcher for several routes.

For Information

Consult your Yellow Pages for local dairies offering milk delivery in your area.

DRIVING

Simply driving a vehicle—an automobile, pickup truck, or van—can earn you part-time profits on a regular basis, either as a chauffeur, taxi driver, deliveryman, or in local transport as a bus or truck driver.

Earnings

Generally over $3 an hour, with tips adding to your income in some cases. The pay will vary greatly depending on whether you are using your own or a company vehicle.

Hours

These will vary so much from one job to another as to be the deciding factor in whether you do the work. Taxi drivers most often are needed in the busy early evening hours through midnight. Part-time charter bus drivers can work days, evenings, Saturday or Sunday, but usually a full day's shift or half shift for evening outings. Deliveries are made most often to customers in the daytime, and to companies by day or night.

Requirements

A license to operate a car, truck, or bus. Sometimes special insurance is needed if you drive your own vehicle commercially, and a good driving record is necessary to get the job. You must be willing to look for this work, perhaps advertise for delivery work for stores and business. Check small, local trucking firms and express delivery outfits and individual wholesalers and retailers who offer delivery. Apply at cab firms. Check airport limousine services. Newspapers need drivers to deliver newspaper bundles to newsboys. Druggists, grocery stores, food take-out services, and liquor retailers are among the many kinds of businesses that offer delivery —or maybe never thought of it until you suggested it!

Future

Owning your own truck or trucks for hire, or operating your own independent delivery or taxi service could result from successfully building up a driving job. Or you can content yourself with a good steady hourly income working for someone else.

For Information

Go through your Yellow Pages and make a list of companies which advertise delivery or have driving as an inherent factor in their service, narrowing down your list to the kinds of driving jobs which suit your circumstances and inclinations. There'll be many, so get on the phone and call them.

WAITRESS, WAITER, HOSTESS

Here is a part-time job which often lends itself ideally to an extra income need, because the busy hours of restaurants are in the evenings, from 5:00 P.M. to midnight, after the regular workday is done. Men and women are needed to greet customers, serve them food and beverages, and to clean up afterwards. If you don't like the idea of waiting on customers, there are the busboy and dishwashing jobs, but the hourly pay is minimum.

Earnings

All restaurant workers who deal with the public generally share in a big bonus of tips, which sometimes add up to more than the basic pay. Cocktail waitresses and fancy restaurant waiters generally get the biggest tips, but it all depends on how crowded the place is. Nevertheless, the basic pay, often a minimum wage, plus tips, averages out to a regular, steady income.

Hours

Usually evenings, from 5:00 to 10:00 P.M. or 6:00 P.M. to 2:00 A.M., depending on the place. Many noon-hour jobs, from about 11:00 A.M. to 2:00 P.M., also are available.

Requirements

Ability to handle food, drinks, and money with swiftness, courtesy, and accuracy. Politeness and giving the customers what they want will influence the size of your tips. Experience is generally not necessary.

Future

A few waiters and waitresses have opened their own restaurants or bars, and although they gained experience in the business from their jobs, the financial investment was the deciding factor. This is a good part-time job that can become a full-time job.

For Information

A restaurant that needs help is more likely to put a small sign in a window than to advertise, so make the rounds, or telephone and ask for the manager.

OFFICE WORK

If you can type, file, operate a business machine, add figures or just answer the telephone and be a receptionist, your service is in demand in many offices and companies of all types, big and small. There are many Kelly Girl or office temporary type of agencies you can sign up with and they find the part-time jobs for you—generally on the basis of one, two, or more days at a time. You can turn down jobs that don't fit your schedule and you collect your pay from the agency, which makes profit from the firm it sent you to. Or you can apply at individual firms yourself for specific or general work.

Earnings

Typists get up to $2.50 an hour, varying according to the section of the country and the individual's experience. Those with lesser or greater business skills are paid comparable rates on a steady basis.

Hours

The greater number of these jobs are for women and require availability during regular business hours, 9:00 A.M. to 5:00 P.M., but this can be one day a week or more, filling in for vacationing or absent workers, or just helping out in a business rush. Many factories, department stores, and service businesses, like trucking firms, fun their offices nightly, too, with half shifts or full shifts available.

Requirements

Experience is needed in typing or specific job categories, but for general office work and filing, receptionist, etc., most firms are willing to show the new employee what must be done. Some familiarity with office procedures is always an asset, of course, and in getting most office jobs a good appearance if a factor.

For Information

Apply at Kelly Girl or similar job agencies where no fee is charged for you, or telephone local businesses which advertise for full-time help and ask the office manager if they would hire you part time, either half days or a few days a week. Smaller firms are more likely to say yes. For evening work, try airlines, trucking firms, hospitals, bus and cab companies, late-hour department stores, automobile sales outlets, and anyone that advertises for inventory help. Check in the Yellow Pages under Employment for agencies handling temporary office help.

HOUSEWORK OR MAID

Much in demand in most areas of the country are persons willing to do a good job of housecleaning, either for working mothers or for motels and hotels, and many part-time opportunities exist. There are agencies specializing in providing house cleaners without fee to the employee and paying on a day-to-day basis. Some even provide transportation. It's the same kind of cleaning and polishing you'd be doing at home, but by doing it for others, you'll see how much it's worth.

Earnings

Pay is generally on a per-day basis, ranging from $15 to $25 a day, depending on whether it's easy work or not, and on the shortage of available help.

Hours

Usually a full day at a time is required, but often there are smaller jobs requiring work for only a half day at a time. Almost always daylight work when dealing with homes.

Requirements

No experience necessary. Sometimes transportation will be needed.

Future

Possible steady full-time work, or good, no-fuss part-time pay.

For Information

Contact domestics and day worker agencies which do not charge you a fee, or telephone local hotels, motels, apartment buildings, and business offices. The latter are ideal for evening work, requiring cleanup after the business day is done. The building manager generally does the hiring.

STORE CLERK

Many retail stores today are geared to stay open for evening hours, and require extra personnel from 5:00 to 10:00 P.M. These include everything from large department stores to small drug stores; liquor stores are open even later in most states. If you would like meeting customers and waiting on them, whether it be shoes or hats they need, then this job could solve any man's or woman's extra income problem.

Earnings

Pay is generally less than $2.50 an hour, but sometimes there is a bonus for a sales quota and often there is the fringe benefit of employee discounts on merchandise.

Hours

Early evening hours, daytime, or Saturdays.

Requirements

Experience is seldom necessary unless the product is highly specialized. Usually goods are price tagged and the clerk needs only to compute sales tax and make change, after assisting the customer in finding what he or she wants.

Future

A full-time job at higher pay could result or, with experience, you could become store manager.

For Information

Look up and telephone department stores, hardware, shoe, dress, and specialty stores, asking for the manager, or apply in person, whether they advertise for help or not. If they know you're interested, they may realize they *could* use extra help.

STOCK CLERK, WAREHOUSEMAN

Behind the scenes of every retail and wholesale operation there is considerable work done to move the right merchandise out to the buyers, and it starts from the point where a railroad car or truck-load of goods arrives at the store or warehouse. Unloading of cases, identifying and shelving them, selecting orders for transfer, reloading operations, pricing and putting the goods on display, all are part of this marketing system and many jobs are open in various phases: dock loaders, fork lift operators, order pickers, shipping clerks, and stockmen all are part of the team required.

Earnings

Range from $2.50 to $3.50 an hour, approximately, varying regionally, depending on job requirements.

Hours

Much night work is available in this field, preparing goods for the next day's business, but often a full eight hours' work at a time is needed, at least several days a week. In loading and stockwork there are more part-time hours open.

Requirements

Most of the jobs in this line call for an able-bodied man, and where paper work is involved, as for shipping clerks, some experience usually is called for. Otherwise, it's just a matter of willingness to work.

Future

Store or warehouse foreman's positions can be achieved by learning specific jobs thoroughly and displaying an eagerness to advance.

For Information

Use your Yellow Pages to look up and telephone large distributors, warehouses, chain store operators, freight outlets, department stores, and supermarkets. Ask for the foreman in charge of hiring.

POSTAL WORKER

There *is* part-time work available with the government, and one notable branch is the U.S. Post Office, which has a seasonal demand for mail handlers, sorters, and carriers. Most of the work is easy to learn and there is a choice of indoor or outdoor jobs.

Earnings

The government pays a good wage, $3.50 or more an hour for even inexperienced workers. And the pay is regular.

Hours

Most often a daytime, Saturday, or evening shift of eight hours at a time is required, and in seasons like Christmas, the post office likes to hire men for full forty-hour weeks, with overtime, on a temporary basis.

Requirements

Generally no experience is required, and the positions, except for heavy labor with big mailbags, are open to both men and women. For some positions a driver's license is needed.

Future

With experience, the possibility of a permanent, good-paying civil service job exists.

For Information

Contact your local postmaster at the post office. In connection with similar jobs, try the county tax collector's office a month before tax bills are scheduled to be mailed out.

BARTENDER

Waiting on customers from behind a bar, serving drinks, and making change, doesn't have to be a skilled occupation if you find a bar limited to beer and wine. You relieve the regular bartender one or two nights a week, and there may be a chance to learn mixing drinks.

Earnings

Usually by the hour, varying from one area to another, but averaging $3.50.

Hours

Depending on local liquor laws, from early evening to midnight or later, an eight-hour shift or less.

Requirements

You must be over 21, in most states, and able to convince the manager you can do the work. If completely inexperienced, offer to work a night free with the regular bartender to learn and show you can do it.

Future

Steady, full-time bartender's work.

For Information

Call local bars. The bartenders can tell you what the hiring situation is, but usually the manager or owner does the hiring.

PLAYGROUND SUPERVISOR, CAMP COUNSELOR

If the after-school hours and Saturday are times you can devote to earning extra money, or if you'll have summer weeks open and like children, a job as playground supervisor or camp counselor might be a pleasurable line of work for you. It's more like play, with yourself in charge of leading fun and games for the youngsters.

Earnings

The pay is not high, generally, but depends on the amount of responsibility and, of course, the hours you work.

Hours

For playgrounds, usually from 3:00 to 5:00 or 6:00 in the afternoon, but in summers and for camp positions, full-time hours are open.

Requirements

Must like working with children, and if you have any experience in athletics or games, it's an asset.

Future

Full-time work as parks director or camp supervisor, if you stick with it.

For Information

Contact your city, county, or state recreation and parks department and inquire about openings and applications. Write to private boys' and girls' camps within convenient travel distance from you.

COLLECTIONS

Here is a versatile job that can be done for almost any company in town for a regular paycheck, or in the spare hours you set, for a commission on whatever you collect. Most merchants have a long list of unpaid bills in their files and would be glad to put someone to work for a chance of bringing in even half the money due. Most people are honest and will agree to pay at least something on an old bill they have let go for too long, if they are approached in a nice way, either by mail or in person.

Earnings

It's possible to make over $50 a week, perhaps $100 or more, either working by the hour or pocketing a fat percentage of every dollar you collect.

Hours

If a merchant hires you he'll probably expect regular hours, perhaps in the late afternoon and early evening; but if you start on a commission basis, you can set your own hours.

Requirements

You must be willing to contact people and talk with them, or communicate clearly and forcefully in letters, and you might have to do a little detective work to find people who have moved. You can work from your home or from a business office.

Future

Many persons who start out collecting bills for others find it's so easy that they set up their own business—$2,500 a year, part time, from their home or $15,000 a year and more, full-time.

For Information

A home course on collecting, leading to your own business, and including even the letters to write to bill owers, is available from Continental Credit Associates, Post Office Box 2023, Des Moines, Iowa 50310. Or telephone doctors, stores, and companies and ask if they need someone to collect old accounts.

BE A MODEL

You don't have to be a five-foot-five, 110-pound beauty to become a model. Character faces, men and women, children, too, are in demand to display a variety of merchandise from clothing to soap powder. The pay is good, but the jobs, frankly, are not regular. If an occasional few hours' work at top level pay are all you need, why not try it.

Earnings

Around $20 an hour can be expected by an experienced photographer's model—though some make five times as much. On the other hand you earn considerbly less working for a local department store.

Hours

Variable. Generally only a few hours at a time, at the employer's convenience.

Requirements

A sense of grace, a smooth walk, and a lack of shyness: you'll be stared at. To be good looking or average looking is a decided asset. Photos of yourself (a portfolio) are often needed, too.

Future

Some models work at top pay all week long, and become cover girls, too. Or television commercials! Not all are filmed in Hollywood and New York; the local shows look for local talent.

For Information

Check your Yellow Pages for modeling agencies; you list with them and they send you on jobs that suit your looks. Or contact a model's school near home for training.

APARTMENT MANAGER

With little work at all required in many cases, you can serve as an apartment building manager, showing the periodic vacancies to potential renters and collecting rent brought to you. Sometimes small maintenance tasks are required. too.

Earnings

For small apartment buildings, your pay is most often in terms of rent, either a reduction or a free apartment, depending on how much work is required of you. But even a free apartment can mean up to $100 a month or more, with little effort.

Hours

You will be required to live on the premises, but this does not mean that your time is not your own. When you go out you just put up a little sign, "The Manager Will Be Back At _____ ."

Requirements

You must be able to move, and the apartment in question must suit your family. For larger buildings where regular maintenance is needed, couples are often sought, with the wife handling the renting and the husband serving as handyman after his regular work hours —for extra pay, of course.

Future

Larger buildings, more income. Perhaps hotel or motel management.

For Information

Inquire by telephone or in person at apartment buildings in areas where you would like to live. If there is no manager's vacancy now, chances are there will be one later.

SWITCHBOARD OPERATOR

Almost every medium-size and large business, apartment building, or motel in town has a need for a switchboard operator, full time and for night relief work. It's easy work, sitting down and handling incoming and outgoing calls. Anyone can learn telephone switchboard operation with a little concentration, and many places will break in a relief operator without experience.

Earnings

The pay is regular, and runs approximately $2.50 an hour. Trainees might make less and experiences operators more.

Hours

A couple of hours at lunchtime or dinner hour, or from a few hours to an entire shift in the evening, depending on the job.

Requirements

Willingness to learn and the ability to work fast and automatically at a simple task. A good speaking voice and a polite manner are assets.

Future

Full-time work or receptionist-PBX jobs.

For Information

Call hotels, motels, large apartment buildings, offices, and businesses. The switchboard operator probably can tell you if help is needed and who is in charge of hiring.

LIFEGUARD

This is strictly seasonal work, available almost everywhere in the country, but it is rewarding work that can mean saving lives, and is not a demanding job except for that occasional emergency. Men and women are hired for positions watching beaches or pools for safety practices and just-in-case.

Earnings

The pay is low because many college-age youths apply for these jobs during their summer vacation, and the hourly rate varies vastly from one area of the country to another, also fluctuating in connection with other services which may be required, such as swimming instruction or conducting first aid classes.

Hours

Generally requires a full day from the first heat of the sun until sunset, but some part-time jobs are available, usually afternoons.

Requirements

If you are a good swimmer and have the knowledge of first aid, or can learn it as it applies to common beach accidents, then these qualifications and general good health are all you'll need besides a bathing suit. Most municipal lifeguard services will require that you pass certain tests which will rate your qualifications from beginner to first class.

Future

Swimming instructor or recreation director jobs can be developed from this initial lifeguard post.

For Information

Contact your local department of parks and beaches, private beach clubs, large motels, wherever there is public swimming in the summer months, and ask about lifeguard work. Big beach lifeguard forces generally have their own training program at the start of the season, so you have to get in your bid early to win this job.

COMPANION TO SHUT-INS

Some disabled persons require non-nursing care or at least a little attention that their friends and relatives are not always able to provide because of distance, their own work, or other responsibilities. Tasks involved might be pushing a wheelchair through a park or just the pleasant playing of a hand of cards, reading a book to the blind, or perhaps just checking regularly by telephone to make sure the ailing person is alright.

Earnings

Vary widely depending on the care required and the hours involved.

Hours

Generally you can establish your own hours, but you must be willing to make adjustments for the convenience of the person involved.

Requirements

No medical knowledge is required, of course, because if there were anything more complicated than procuring a medicine bottle from its shelf, then a nurse or doctor would be called. If you are interested in people and feel a need to be needed, this can be very rewarding work, with the extra bonus of new friendship.

Future

Some full-time companion positions are open, including travel abroad with wealthy persons.

For Information

Talk to the person in charge at a local hospital, sanitarium, or nursing office and ask about cases where medical assistance is not required but some companionship is necessary.

CROSSING GUARD

Many schools regularly employ persons to stop traffic at crosswalks and lead children across the street at morning, noon, and afternoon, little more than an hour at a time.

Earnings

Pay is hourly and not very large, but it is regular each week, except during the summer.

Hours

Generally from an hour before school starts in the morning to the beginning bell, with similar coverage of the lunch hour, and then from a few minutes before school is out until an hour or more later. It usually amounts to a maximum of four hours a day, twenty hours a week, but the schools are often flexible enough to hire crossing guards for only a few days, or partial shifts if necessary.

Requirements

Good vision (with glasses is okay) and general alertness, with common sense and awareness of local vehicle and pedestrian traffic regulations.

Future

Limited, part-time work only.

For Information

Telephone or write to large and small public and private schools in your neighborhood or in any area where you would like to work, or contact your local Board of Education for information about pay rates, hours, and applications.

LIBRARIAN

If you like books and reading, the local library may be the place for you—either waiting on people and recommending books, or stocking the shelves in front or back. It's easy, regular work and most libraries are willing to hire persons part time, a few hours a day.

Earnings

Low, hourly rate, but there is the benefit of training for higher pay professional librarian's work.

Hours

Adjustable, depending on employer. Most libraries are willing to employ persons morning, afternoon, or evening, a half day at a time, depending on their needs.

Requirements

Reading ability, for titles and placement of books in their proper location, and an ability to meet the public. You will have to learn the library numbering system, too.

Future

Professional librarian's work, with sufficient experience and some training, can result from a starting part-time job.

For Information

Contact by telephone your local library or department of libraries and ask about job openings and applications. Note also, book stores frequently offer similar work at slightly higher pay, so don't overlook them if the library has no openings.

NEWSPAPER DELIVERY

Even home-to-home delivery of newspapers or advertising tabloids can be a profitable adult's work if it's done on a large enough scale, perhaps using an auto to make the rounds.

Earnings

Only a few cents at the most per paper delivered, but a route of several hundred dwellings, homes, or apartment units, can make the small fee add up quickly, and the pay is regular, a little every day.

Hours

Morning papers usually are delivered by dawn, so a big route might mean starting at 3:00 in the morning or earlier, while afternoon paper delivery often starts about 1:00 P.M. and continues until about 6:00 P.M., when the last deliveries should be done. Daily and Sunday.

Requirements

For a large route, transportation. Otherwise, all you need is the ability to keep track of where the customers live and when they pay.

Future

Distributorships may open up.

For Information

Contact your local and largest area newspapers or advertising firms which offer home delivery of tabloids.

RESERVATIONS CLERK

Airlines, bus depots, train stations, rent-a-car stations, and similar transportation facilities need people to take their calls, meet their customers, fill out tickets, and make change. Usually the jobs are available day and night, because the services are around the clock; but there are definite rush hours, like the weekend travel surge. If you can greet people with a friendly smile, consult simplified rate and destination charts, and take the money required after issuing the proper tickets, there may be a part-time spot for you in one of these behind-the-counter jobs.

Earnings

Pay generally is at an hourly rate exceeding $3 an hour; much more for busy spots and experienced clerks.

Requirements

Must like to meet people and deal with them as a representative of a large, public relations-conscious firm, and have a willingness to learn the ever-changing schedules and rates that apply to all transportation facilities.

Hours

Day or evening, anywhere from a full eight-hour shift to an hour at a time meeting incoming aircraft late at night, or preparing for an isolated departure. Depends on local conditions and needs of firm.

Future

Full-time reservations clerks or managers who know their systems' every detail command a good salary and can grow with the ever-expanding transportation business.

For Information

Telephone individual airlines, bus companies, railroad lines, and auto rental firms serving your community and ask the manager what the job prospects might be.

USHER, AMUSEMENT OPERATOR

Here are two easy jobs in the amusement industry, one of them regular and the other usually temporary, but otherwise much the same. Basically you are serving the public which comes for entertainment or amusement. Ushers shine a flashlight and show people to their seats, while an amusement booth operator or ride conductor more closely controls the amusement.

Earnings

A low, hourly rate, regular in the case of ushers, temporary in the case of amusement operators for traveling carnivals, etc.

Hours

Afternoons and evenings, anywhere from a few hours to ten, depending on the employer's needs and your availability.

Requirements

No experience necessary in most cases. In dealing with carnival rides and booths, operators usually are broken in locally before the first customers arrive.

Future

Strictly part-time or temporary work, but many theater managers or show entrepreneurs start this way.

For Information

Telephone film and stage theaters in your area, as well as permanent amusement parks, or show up in person on the first night or morning of arrival of a circus or carnival.

Chapter 4
A SERVICE THAT PAYS

You don't have to make anything or sell any product to earn good supplementary income. One of the best opportunities for part-time profit lies in performing a service that people want and are willing to pay someone else to do. Often they *must* pay someone else, either because they lack the know-how, the tools, the ability, or the time to perform the task themselves.

Performing a service to customers has the advantage of very flexible hours, since each job is initiated with an agreement between you and the buyer as to when and where you will do the work involved. Often, there is little investment required because you are not dealing in a product; but some tools may be necessary, since this is one reason the customer comes to you to do the work rather than doing it himself. Inherent in this, of course, is the fact that often a skill or special know-how on your part is what you really are selling. Highly paid plumbers, electricians, or just handymen make their living because of their knowledge and handiness with the tools of their trade. But, chances are, if you are seeking part-time work, you already have some special skill from your regular job, or from a past job or course of vocational instruction you may have taken. If so, you can transfer your regular job's skill to your spare time profits simply by advertising or otherwise letting people know you are available for such work on a per-job basis.

Even lacking any particular trade or skill that will adapt to part-time jobs, there are many opportunities for service work which require only the basic tool, such as a rug shampoo machine, floor waxer, lawn mower, picture framing kit, tool sharpener, or just a small truck. All of these can be rented or purchased locally. And who couldn't perform such services as baby-sitting or yard cleanup without even a basic tool investment?

Many service jobs can be performed right in your own home, with the customer bringing the job to you, which is another appeal of service work. Again, the listings that follow do not pretend to be all inclusive, and, because of some special aspect of individual work fields, you will find many possible service opportunities listed in other chapters. For those who have no special skill to capitalize on in the line of service, the chapter on learning profitable occupations will be especially worthwhile reading.

Here are a wide variety of things you can do for others to solve your own financial problems:

TYPEWRITER REPAIRS

With the continuing growth of offices and paperwork, thousands of new typewriter repairmen are needed every year just to keep the machines working properly. Work from your own home, garage, or basement, or work for big office companies or small local business machine dealers.

Earnings

With your own business you can earn $20 an hour and more in your spare time, or even full time. Or hire out as a trained technician with a respected specialty, for craftsman's pay of $5 an hour or more.

Hours

If you work for yourself you can set your own hours, a couple a day or ten to forty hours a week or more. Taking a job with others will require more regular work, but such technicians are so much in demand that companies usually will be glad to hire you for a day, a week, afternoons, or a few hours in the evenings.

Requirements

This job requires a skill, of course, but you can learn it at home in your spare time, or apply as a trainee at a local typewriter repair shop. You'll also need a few basic manuals and a dozen small tools to go with the know-how.

Future

Depending on local competition, and generally there is plenty of work to go around, you could start your own repair shop at home or in a rented store. Or a typewriter sales store might be glad to provide you free work space and give you the business of taking care of all their customers.

For Information

Write Typewriter Repair School, Department 3110-019, Little Falls, New Jersey 07424.

INTERIOR DECORATING

If you possess good taste and basic color sense, and are willing to learn, you can become an interior decorator, helping homeowners and apartment developers to make their rooms look as attractive as they want. You can work out of your home or out of somebody else's furniture or fabric store, and you can take on as many or as few jobs as you wish. It is likeable, creative work that can be mastered at home.

Earnings

Interior decorators often don't charge a penny for their services, but they collect a commission on all the furniture and fabrics that customers buy through them at beneficial wholesale prices. Or furniture and furnishings stores hire you at a regular salary as a service for their customers. The pay is good, about $150 a week working for yourself.

Hours

If you hire out to a merchant, they will expect regular business hours to be maintained, although it is common for interior decorators to work only part time, either on the busy store weekends, a few days a week, or by appointment. If you run your own service, your time will be your own, but better count on more than a day a week.

Requirements

A sense of style and beauty, plus a willingness to consult with and please the customers at all costs. You must keep abreast of what is fashionable and what is available in furnishings, and their prices. Sketching ability is a decided asset. You must be free to visit homes and shop in stores all over town.

Future

Five-figure incomes, even on a part-time basis are not unusual in this business, which has wide open possibilities for the person who wants some day to open his own establishment. Some decorators even manufacture their own furniture, draperies, and objects of art, doubling their profits.

For Information

Write Chicago School of Interior Decoration, 835 Diversey Parkway, Chicago, Illinois 60614, about their home-study, diploma course. Or contact local schools through the Yellow Pages or the home economics department of the public schools, adult education division.

RUN A GARAGE SALE

If you are good at organizing, you can profit by operating a continuing garage sale at your residence, offering for sale all the used furniture, toys, clothes, appliances, and other things that you, your neighbors, and friends want to sell. Your customers benefit with bargains, and they come to you!

Earnings

You should establish a 10 to 20 per cent commission which you collect from all sales of other people's goods. Profits can vary from a few dollars to $50 a week, depending on how many people come and buy.

Hours

Whatever hours you set for the sale, either every day or every weekend, you will have to be available at home to meet customers; but most of the time you can be doing other things—even fixing up some sale articles so they'll bring a better price.

Requirements

Zoning restrictions applying to commerce generally do not affect such an operation among friends and neighbors, but better check. Otherwise all you need is the ambition, the space, and a little want-ad or supermarket advertising.

Future

Used furniture stores have started this way. Everybody loves a bargain.

For Information

Ask your friends and neighbors, or a woman's club, if they have the articles to sell and are willing. Check newspaper prices for new and used articles so your bargains will bring buyers.

HOME MOVING

You don't even have to own a truck to get into this big service business. More people than ever before are moving to new addresses, so there is plenty of business in helping them pack and transport their belongings safely. Contracts with new home sellers, real estate agents, and apartment managers can help find you business. The truck? You rent it only when you need it.

Earnings

The rates for moving are regulated in many states, usually on a per-hour basis with considerations for mileage, but the allowed rate (call movers and ask) comes to over $10 an hour.

Hours

This is strictly a customer's choice, and almost always a daylight job. Even smaller jobs will take as much as a half day. Loading, driving, and unloading. Weekends, particularly Saturdays, are the biggest moving days, so you'd better be free.

Requirements

You'll need strength, a helper for the bigger household items, a driver's license, and the ability to handle a small truck. A truck, a dolly or two, and furniture padding must be available, but these can be rented in most cities. For weekends, though, you'll have to plan ahead and reserve them. And you'll have to solicit business by advertising or just letting enough people know you're available.

Future

If you can set aside enough of the profits of a part-time moving business to put a down payment on your own truck, you've got your own business. Promote it and you'll soon have two trucks—driven by people you hire.

For Information

Contact your local office of the Public Utilities Commission or other regulatory agencies. Check your Yellow Pages for big interstate movers who offer booklets on their service.

LINOLEUM, TILE, AND CARPET LAYING

Here is a skill that many product distributors will be willing to teach you if you use their products. Home improvement is such big business today that you'll only be idle when you choose to be. The work is not strenuous. It is quiet and usually solitary, and it gives the satisfaction of a job well done; yet the products have advanced to such a stage that most are sold to do-it-yourself–ers with more ambition than skill. Almost anyone can learn, but practice makes perfect. Your customers will be those who are unwilling, unable, or too busy to do it themselves.

Earnings

You can charge $1 a yard for carpet laying, pennies a foot for tile, but it will average about $5 an hour once you learn to work with confidence. There is also profit in the material, since if you offer and sell certain products from samples, you can demand a commission from the supplier. Or you can work regularly, part or full time, for a little less an hour, for a dealer.

Hours

Usually customers will ask when you can do it and you'll be able to set your hours to a certain degree. This is usually a daytime or early evening job, and even the smallest installation will require several hours in a row.

Requirements

If you are willing to do manual labor, can learn to work with your hands quickly, and are able to negotiate with carpet and tile dealers as well as attract customers, you can handle this trade profitably. A few small tools are needed, too.

Future

Building a business from this trade will require initiative. Finding the customers can be the most difficult part, but if you can line up a whole new housing development, market center, or apartment building to bolster what may be a seasonal factor in the business in some areas, then you're practically an independent contractor, and you'll earn a full-time, five-figure income, profiting on the labor of those you hire and the products you buy at wholesale.

For Information

Consult your Yellow Pages for tile, linoleum, and carpet dealers as an initial step, and be willing to work by the hour at laborer's pay while you learn, if necessary. If you pursue the work beyond a part-time scale, check on union regulations and government requirements for building trade contractors.

CLEAN UPHOLSTERY

Here is another unique business for the man who has little or no training, but a great deal of ambition: run your own upholstery cleaning business. Machines are available from specialty firms which enable you to clean upholstery right on the customer's premises, in homes, business offices, motels, etc. You operate from your own home, using your own car, and the only investment needed is the machine and a special cleaning fluid.

Earnings

You set your own prices and hours, so earnings are strictly up to you, limited only by your eagerness to work. Some upholstery cleaning machine owners report averaging $100 a day, most of it clear profit.

Hours

You probably could pretty much choose your own working hours, but if you go after the big-paying jobs like hotels, motels, and business offices, they may dictate the hours you can work—often at night in the case of businesses. Count on a few hours per job, but you can work one job a day or one a week, five a day or five a week, as you wish.

Requirements

No special training is necessary, although you should have enough nerve to get on the telephone and call people you don't know, offering to clean their upholstery. Sometimes a newspaper ad will bring the customers calls to you. Place a business card on shopping center bulletin boards for housewives, and drop in at motels and office buildings. Complete instructions on operations, including business manuals and consultation service, is supplied by the maker of the machines, which can be purchased with a small down payment that will be quickly earned back.

For Information

Write Von Schrader Manufacturing Corporation, 9911 "D" Place, Racine, Wisconsin 53403. Or look in your Yellow Pages for similar companies closer to home.

SPECIALIZE IN WATERPROOFING

There is hardly an area in America where at least seasonal problems of water leakage don't crop up, flooding basements and homes and costing the owners hundreds of dollars in damages. Yet, if you know how, waterproofing a basement or other vulnerable structure is relatively easy. There are a number of products on the market which can do the job, among them a glazed, sand-cement mortar which is applied over concrete or brick walls and seals them immediately, even if they had already started to seep water. Just common sense ability and a willingness to work are all you need to get started, really, because the work is simple, healthy, and rewarding. And you may be the only one in town offering this special service.

Earnings

You can earn from $25 to $100 for a single job, depending on the size of the basement or wall or other structure that has to be waterproofed. A $25 job could be done in a few hours time, while it might take two days to finish a $100 job. Materials will cost only about $5 per $25 job. One a day or one a week, figure out what your income will be!

Hours

If it's raining out you had better be available, because it is human nature to wait until something leaks before fixing it, but generally you can set your own hours, doing a job in the evening or on week-ends if you start on a limited basis. It will take a minimum of a few hours to do a good job on an average size basement, so you've got to have that much time available in a single stretch.

Requirements

The labor involved in waterproofing is something that can be done by any able bodied man who isn't afraid of getting his hands dirty. You'll have to let people know what your specialty is, either by going around and talking to them or by advertising in the local newspaper. In areas where heavy, damaging rains are strictly sea-sonal, you will have to be willing to go out and drum up jobs in the slack months, perhaps visiting recently flooded areas and passing out your business card with an estimate and a discount. You'll need work clothes, a few common tools, the sealing mix and transporta-tion, but there is a lot of money to be made in this good, honest work that helps a lot of people.

Future

There are some companies that operate a year round waterproof-ing business on a full-time basis, so the job could develop into a firm of your own. But in many parts of the country you would have to add a couple of other related sidelines for the dry seasons, like patching and repairing concrete, painting, or, if you want to really make waterproofing your specialty, you could branch out into other solutions and offer raincoat waterproofing for summer showers, or fix roofs and leaky windows. The income potential is there for the man who can expand and pace this work over the years.

For Information

Instructions, materials and advice are available from the makers of one such compound, Chem-X: Write National Potteries Com-pany, 1126 Third Avenue East, Grand Rapids, Minnesota.

INSTALL FORMICA

Countertops in every kitchen and den and articles of furniture that get utilitarian wear can spell big profits for you in this specialty, and it's one in which others will find the customers for you.

Earnings

As your own boss you can set a competitive per-foot charge for installations, one that should bring you better than journeyman car-penter's pay of approximately $5 an hour.

Hours

It's pretty much a daylight hours job, but you can have some flexibility, working a few hours at a time on weekends or early evenings only, if you wish. But people will be in a hurry to have the work done, so you'll have to be able to stick with a job until it's finished.

Requirements

A little skill with common tools and the ability to learn will get you into this profitable sideline. Many appliance dealers find themselves with whole kitchen remodeling jobs on their hands and are glad to find someone they can present with the craftsmanship work. But you'll have to seek them out and ask. And advertise.

Future

In some locales where building and remodeling are brisk enough, particularly in bigger cities, there is room for a specialty countertop shop, but in most cases you'd have to be prepared to expand into other materials, like ceramic tiles, to make it a profitable full-time business.

For Information

Write Japs, 126 Seventh Street North, Hopkins, Minnesota 55343.

INSTALL BURGLAR ALARMS

In these days of violence, security is big business, and more and more private homes are putting in their own burglar alarms. No electrical license or experience is required, and the company that makes the alarm systems will actively drum up the sales for you. It's not a door-to-door sales job. You place special foil strips along windows, levers at door jambs, and pieces of metal on window sills, linking them with a wire to a bell. One very good source of business is the neighborhood that has just been visited by a burglar! Direct mail pieces will bring in plenty of inquiries.

Earnings

Take one common installation as an example; ten points of possible entry. Your cost of materials is about $15. Suggested charge is $90, for a profit of $75 on a single job. You can keep a client list and charge regular monthly service fees that add up, too.

Hours

Generally you will have to work in daylight hours for the sake of visibility while installing, but some jobs can be done at night, especially in busy stores. Be sure to clear night installations with the local police, especially before testing the alarm! You can do one job in a few hours' work.

Requirements

You should be handy with common tools, and enjoy working as an insider on the side of the law with the approval of the local police. You probably will be issued a badge to clear you for your work with local authorities. A shoestring investment is required for the tools and equipment, which fit easily into an auto trunk. Direct selling won't be necessary, but you'll have to advertise your much-in-demand service, either through mail or newspapers.

Future

Many persons can make a full-time occupation or even a big business out of burglar alarm installation, taking in $12,000 to $20,000 a year on a forty-hour week basis. It is a respected field with plenty of prestige and profits for those who are willing to work at it regularly and learn all the ins and outs of the business. But before you jump into this intriguing operation, check your local Yellow Pages or Chamber of Commerce to see if there is much competition, and if you can beat their prices.

For Information

A full starter kit of materials and instructions for every step are available from Nasco, 11071 Massachusetts Avenue, Los Angeles, California 90025. Or apply at burglar alarm companies which advertise in your local area.

BE A LOCKSMITH

Picking locks, installing them, or making keys, freeing people from locked rooms, or getting them into their locked homes and cars, is an art that mystifies most people, thus making the locksmith in any town a respected craftsman. But actually, almost anyone who can work with tools and has a steady hand for dealing with tiny objects can master this craft and make a secure and profitable living from it. Generally this is a job for a self-starter, whether he pursues it full time or part time. The more than three hundred tools of the trade are the secret; they really do the work.

Earnings

Some beginners report averaging $3 to $10 an hour in their spare time, while learning, and those who set up their own shops, either in their homes or in a small, rented downtown store, come closest to the higher figure. And it's almost 100 per cent profit.

Hours

Variable. This job can be placed on a regular workday basis if you concentrate on installing and replacing locks and key-making, and there are always many jobs that can be done in spare time at home. But there will always be emergency calls, too, and these can mean an hour's rush work at any time of day or night.

Requirements

If you can concentrate on simple diagrams, follow instructions, and handle small tools, you can learn this trade quickly, studying in your free time at home and gaining practical experience by working with actual car locks, home locks, safe locks, and padlocks. You'll also need a car for transportation, of course.

Future

Some large-traffic supermarket and department stores are glad to set up a locksmith with the space he needs, just for the service to their customers, although they will expect a commission or rent for their ideal situation. But opening your own shop is a distinct future calling, and you can double your earnings by selling locks, keys, and safety devices, too.

For Information

Write Locksmithing Institute, Little Falls, New Jersey 07424.

APPLIANCE REPAIRS

Every home today is filled with electrical gadgets from can openers and percolators to washing machines and refrigerators, and sooner or later they tend to break down. That's when the appliance repairman is called, and if you are in this profitable line of work you have the satisfaction of performing a truly needed service that people gladly pay for. It's simple. Who wouldn't pay $25 to a repairman for fixing the washer, rather than replacing it for $200 or more? Even if it only took him an hour! Work out of your home, in a corner of the basement, or in the garage.

Earnings

Full or part time, you can count on an income of $4 to $6 an hour if you drum up a regular flow of customers and work for yourself at home. For major appliance home repair calls, of course, the rate is more than double, and you can profit on parts, too. Or you can work for an appliance sales store on a regular hourly wage.

Hours

If you set up appliance repair as your own independent business, you can pace yourself with a one-hour job per day, a few jobs on the weekends or evenings, of whatever you want, all the way up to full time. If you can be available on an emergency basis, when refrigerators or air conditioners break down, and do rush repairs, you'll profit all the more.

Requirements

You'll have to have a good mechanical sense to handle this craft, but if you have a knowledge of car engines or just like to take things apart and put them together again, this may be the job for you. Manuals and the right tools make many difficult tasks easy. Transportation, tools, and a workbench also are needed.

Future

This job can develop into either a full forty to forty-eight-hour workweek for somebody else, or you can go into business for yourself with your own shop. There are 800 million appliances in the country, about a dozen to a home, so there is plenty of work available for the repairman who can help keep them going.

For Information

Write Appliance Division, National Radio Institute, 3939 Wisconsin Avenue, Washington, D.C. 20016.

SMALL ENGINE REPAIRS

In your spare time you can salvage outboard motors, power mowers, chain saws, and similar equipment, which people tend to let rust away when they fail. Whether you offer repair work as a service or purchase broken equipment for a few dollars and restore it for resale, this can be a worthwhile sideline that will keep extra dollars pouring in.

Earnings

You can earn $5 an hour and more on repair jobs customers bring to you, working in your garage or basement. If a $50 power mower breaks down, no one questions a $10 repair bill, even if you just had to clean out the gas line.

Hours

Set your own. Work nights or weekends, but for some reason people, tend to wait until weekends to bring the work in. Most will wait a week to get it back, so you can adjust your time.

Requirements

You have to be handy with tools and willing to learn and experiment. Recognizing the problem in engine repair is half the work, and there are tools and tests that help you do this. Work in your garage or basement, or drive to the customer's place.

Future

Dealing in sales of secondhand outboards, power mowers, and similar small-engine equipment is the natural expansion for a repairman in this field, so you could set up your own regular store and profit on your sales as well as your craft. Or there are full-time openings with the product sales outlets and distributors at good, steady wages.

For Information

Write Lincoln Technical Institute, Suite 1-E, 427 Market Street, Newark, New Jersey.

WATCH REPAIRS

This is clean, delicate work with fine instruments and an inexperienced man or woman can learn the craft and set up shop in a space no larger than a desk drawer at home. Many jewelry sales outlets are eager to hire the person who can provide this service for their customers, and they will pay well. Patience, a steady hand, and a sharp eye are assets.

Earnings

Watch repairing will pay at least $5 an hour, even just for cleaning the mechanisms, and if you solicit business from jewelers or the general public and work at home, you can pretty much adjust your earnings according to the amount of work you take.

Hours

Working out of your home, you set your own schedule for a few hours work a day or only a few a week. If you take a job with a jeweler, chances are he will want you at his shop at least during the busy weekend hours.

Requirements

You'll need the ability to study diagrams and handle tiny tools, but once you've mastered one watch, you've got the basic knowledge you need. You'll also have to advertise or solicit business from small jewelry shops, unless you go to work for one exclusively.

Future

An investment in low-cost imported watches can set you up in your own shop for sales as well as repairs, and the customers keep coming back; but this could end up costing a great deal since people expect watch sales outlets to carry a full line of jewelry. Full-time employment with an established jeweler or manufacturer would be a more easily reachable goal; the pay is good and it's steady.

For Information

Write Chicago School of Watchmaking, Department 119, Fox River Grove, Illinois 60021.

PIANO TUNING

Men and women can perform this service, which is more easily learned than one would think, by new, step-by-step pictorial methods and the right few tools. You don't even have to know how to play, but it helps if you have a good ear for music. It is a respected craft that takes you to the best homes for an hour's work or more at a time.

Earnings

You can make up to $10 an hour as an independent piano tuner, and since you will remind customers they should have their piano tuned periodically, there will be consistent repeat business.

Hours

When you work, allowing an hour or more (sometimes a lot more) per job will have to be arranged between yourself and the customer, at your mutual convenience; but even if you only do a few jobs a week it can be a worthwhile side income.

Requirements

If you can follow instructions and have a mechanical inclination as well as an ear for musical scales, you can handle this job. No burdensome tools and not even a workbench are needed for this specialty, since you always work where the piano is. One caution; if yours is a small town with few pianos and there is already a well known tuner, your business will be limited.

Future

Getting enough business is the key, but if you can attract customers, piano tuning as a sideline can be turned into a full-time occupation with very high remuneration. There are tricks to the trade, of course. Solicit business from piano sellers, places where sheet music is sold, or lessons given. Or combine tuning with another sideline like refinishing and restoring old pianos to like-new condition.

For Information

Write Van Brook Company, Oregon, Illinois 61061.

SHARPEN SAWS AND TOOLS

This is an easy, at-home occupation that requires a corner of a workbench and a little ambition. There is plenty of work. Think: how many dull knives, scissors, and other tools do you have around the house that you wish were back in their like-new condition? Every home is a prospect and if you can attract the business, you can earn as little or as much as you like.

Earnings

Income is very irregular, depending on how much work you do, but it's a cash operation and every tool you finish is money in your pocket. People usually bring more than one to two knives, so even at a small charge per piece, you can be making several dollars in a half hour's work.

Hours

In this service, your hours are your own, but if you are advertising for customers it is best that you are around the house, occupied with something else, perhaps, when they come. You can sharpen a dozen small tools well in an hour, but customers usually like to bring the work, wait, and take it home with them. You can make your hours more flexible if you offer pickup and delivery, and you'll probably get more customers, but they will expect fast service.

Requirements

You will need the basic sharpening machine, which requires an initial investment, and the space for working in your garage or basement. Learning to operate the machines is simple by following their guidelines. Getting people into action, making them dig out their dull tools for restoration, is the key to success in this sideline, and advertising is usually what it takes. Some enterprising people have mounted the machine in the back of a pickup truck and gone door-to-door, a service so needed and appreciated that people can't resist.

Future

There is little overhead and all the income is profit, so this can develop into a steady sparetime income of $20, $30 a week or more with little effort, and the work is not hard. With effort, of course, you can attract more business and more money—from markets, restaurants, barber shops, beauticians, and industries; so in the right situation it could become full-time self-employment.

For Information

Write Treyco Products, Inc., 381 Niagara Street North, Tonawanda, New York 14120. Or Foley Manufacturing Company, 116-9 Foley Building, Minneapolis, Minnesota 55418.

BE A DETECTIVE

A glamorous pursuit that means high pay and community respect for diligent operators. Nearly every community has need for this service for a variety of delicate tasks. You may not be chasing criminals all day long, but it is surprising how many individuals and companies hire discreet detective services for finding runaway sons and daughters, tracing threatening letters, recovering lost valuables, checking on employee job applications, and the like. For men or women.

Earnings

Expenses of $50 a day are common in detective work, with another $50 as straight pay, depending on the job. If an employer asks for a routine police record check on two dozen job applicants, the task is simple and the price should encourage business. Depending on results, you can demand the pay you want.

Hours

This is strictly a buyer's market when it comes to hours. You will have to be available any hour of the day or night, sometimes, as in surveillances, for long stretches; but you only have to take the jobs you wish, and to that extent you can be selective about your time.

Requirements

Intelligent, over twenty-one, and tactful; that describes the basic qualifications of a person willing to learn this professional work. You also should like working with people, because many jobs will require just going around and asking a lot of questions. It's not all excitement, but there can be plenty!

Future

Opening your own full-time detective agency with diploma on the wall and regular work coming in is a definite prospect for the person who can demonstrate ability in this science and complete an accredited course. And, for more secure income, there are many large stores, hotels, and industries that hire their own detectives for security purposes and other delicate chores.

For Information

Write Institute of Applied Science, 1920 Sunnyside Avenue, Chicago, Illinois 60640.

SECURITY GUARD OR MERCHANT PARTROLMAN

Any honest man of good character and background can qualify for this worthwhile service with a minimum of training. You watch stores and industries during their off-hours so the job adapts ideally to moonlighting. The evening hours or weekends are when the service is most in demand. You patrol one area after another, just keeping your eyes open. You work in cooperation with your local police. You wear a uniform and badge, and carry a revolver.

Earnings

If you operate an independent security guard service, you can make $500 a month or more working nights and weekends by yourself, or employ others and profit by their work, too.

Hours

Nights and weekends are the key hours when security guards work, driving from store to store on a route or patrolling a housing development or industrial complex on foot. You can do part-time work for some employers who hire guards on a night-by-night basis.

Requirements

Conscientiousness and reliability are musts, but otherwise any man can run his own merchant patrol or hire out to others as a security gard. Size is not important, but alertness and mature judgment are, since you will be watching business establishments and their valuable merchandise to protect them from burglary, theft, and vandalism. Uniform, gun, and car usually are necessary, but if you work for a merchant patrol, these may be provided.

Future

You can build up a route of customers so that you have to hire two or more other persons to adequately patrol the area. If so, you'll be in private business collecting regular fees from every firm you serve.

For Information

Write National Private Patrol Service, Box 327, Springfield, Oregon 97477.

PROFESSIONAL MASSAGE

An easily learned profession allied to the medical arts can be a profitable part-time occupation for a skilled operator, either working out of his home on in connection with doctors, hospitals, clubs, and health centers. You perform a satisfying, healthful service for patients who need relief from aches and pains, or just a stimulating, relaxing uplift.

Earnings

Most masseurs charge about $5 for a one-hour treatment, and the income can be earned on a full-time or part-time basis, so the total pay will fluctuate.

Hours

You can work evenings for an executives end-of-the-day health and exercise club, or weekends in similar recreation centers. Or you can build your own select clientele at any hours convenient to yourself and your customers.

Requirements

Anyone can learn, but you will need enough self-confidence to put the customers at their ease, and you must be willing and able to travel to client's homes or work outside your own home in clubs, etc.—unless, of course, you can set up a professional-looking room at home and attract clients there.

Future

Generally this is not a full-time big business, although some persons have built up whole clinics with half a dozen masseurs working for them; so it can be done. But working regularly with a club or clinic can deliver a steady income on a part-time basis.

GRAPHOANALYSIS

This is an art that has to be learned, but anyone who can study a book can do it. Interpretation of character through a person's handwriting has intrigued millions of people and they are your potential customers. It's fun and fascinating.

Earnings

You can charge $.50 to $1 per signature for this service, depending on how thorough a job you will be doing, and on what the traffic will bear.

Hours

Completely your own decision, if you work entirely from your home. If you set up a stand at the beach, a carnival, or shopping centers, you'll have to abide by their busiest hours if you want plenty of customers.

Requirements

A convincing manner and a serious approach to the art are all that's required. A little ad in your local paper or a national magazine can bring you hundreds of requests by mail, or if you prefer meeting the people, you will have to go where the crowds are.

The Future

If you earn a reputation for interesting, accurate analyses, and discover a steady source of patronage, you can build up a steady, free-time income for work you will enjoy.

For Information
Write Igas, Inc., 325 Jackson, Chicago, Illinois 60606.

LANDSCAPING, LAWN CARE, TREE TRIMMING

Often all three services are rolled into one, but any of them can be pursued as a part-time endeavor. The work is healthy, outdoors in the sun, dealing with beauty in plants and flowers. If you don't mind getting your hands dirty and have a "green thumb" you can build up a good sound route that will pay big dividends.

Earnings

This is seasonal work in most parts of the country, but even a day a week can bring you from $20 to $50, depending on whether you simply mow lawns and trim them, or select, sell, and plant expensive shrubs and small trees to suit your own rough design sketches.

Hours

Daylight is the only restriction on hours, so long as it's all right with your customers. You may offer weekly or bimonthly lawn mowing, regular tree and bush trimming, to whatever extent your time is available, if only on weekends.

Requirements

A little know-how about lawn care and feeding along with an eye for attractive layouts and combinations of palms, evergreens, shrubs, flowers, ivy, rocks, and other landscaping materials, plus transportation will give you wide latitude in this occupation. Tools like mowers, shears, pruners, edgers, and hoses will be required if you go at it in a big way.

Future

Many people have built up extensive routes they serve regularly, perhaps an hour per job per week. With enough of them, it can be a full-time independent business, just in lawn care or seasonal tree trimming. If you learn and promote landscaping, the profits are multiplied considerably, since a landscaping contractor is to the outdoors what the interior decorator is to inside. Big businesses, city buildings, and housing developments hire the landscaping contractors for big sums and since they also profit on the plants they install, they are in the five-figure income bracket easily.

For Information

Call a big local landscaping contractor listed in the Yellow Pages. Or write Lifetime Career Schools, 2251 Barry Avenue, Los Angeles, California 90064.

SOIL TESTING

If this sounds like a complex science, don't be fooled. Many people have trouble growing a good lawn or flowers and they don't understand what the trouble is. Often it's the soil: it has too much of one element or not enough of another. You use a soil testing kit which immediately tells what's wrong, and you've solved their problem.

Earnings

You can charge $3 to $5 per test (the soil may differ from front yard to back) and since your materials cost you only $1 per test, the rest is profit. Your earnings will depend on how much work you can attract.

Hours

Daylight; but that is the only restriction, since an individual test can be made in a few minutes.

Requirements

The only necessity is interest and the ability to attract or go after customers. You will need a soil testing kit, available at any garden shop for $2.98, with enough chemicals for three tests. Anyone can perform the tests after reading the enclosed instructions.

The Future

This is strictly seasonal, part-time work, but perhaps in connection with landscaping, sales can build up a business by supplying the elements and care the soil requires, as well as the plants the improved soil can nourish.

For Information

Visit your local garden shop and ask about soil testing kits, or write to the nearest office of the Department of Agriculture for their pamphlet on the subject.

BE A MORTGAGE BROKER

This is no daydream. What if you could find a part-time job that could earn you up to $10,000 a year or more, with no selling involved, and no special talents that are beyond any normal learning capacity? Impossible? No; many people are doing this as mortgage brokers. Simplified, the job is this: you find people who need large sums of money for financing sound investments like building projects, housing developments, or subdivisions. They need financing, so you make contacts with companies that need investments.

Then bring them together with the answer to their problems. Most mortgage brokers establish themselves as representatives of one or more mortgage lending companies which are seeking solid business loans; the broker examines the proposed project, the assets and projected income, and the amount of money desired, then places the application with the lending company. If the loan is approved, the broker collects a commission which may be as small as 1 per cent. That's not small business, however, if it's a $1,700,000 loan for a 200-unit apartment building, because the commission on that one loan would be $17,000. Interested? Read on.

Earnings

Can range up to 7 per cent on loans you place, depending on terms, but if you only placed one small loan of $50,000 in a month's part-time effort, you have earned $500—actually more, because the smaller the loan, the higher the fee.

Hours

Business hours are generally mandatory unless you meet businessmen at their golf clubs or socially. Otherwise, your hours are your own choice and the prospect's.

Requirements

An understanding of finance, which can be learned by anyone who knows simple addition and multiplication. You also must be able to talk to people and examine the prospects of their projects. They will be trying to sell you on the merits of the investment, because they are the ones who need the loan you may be able to place for them.

Future

Unlimited income and stature. Possible wise investment openings for yourself.

For Information

Write United Mortgage Company, 319 Pat Mell Center, Marietta, Georgia 30060.

TOY CLINIC

If you are good at fixing things, like your own children's toys, why not set up a clinic for repairing other's toys at a profit? The work is simple and satisfying, can be done on a workbench at home, and requires only general handiness.

Earnings

You set your own prices for your service. You can fix a flat tire on a bicycle in ten minutes for $1, or replace a broken part in an hour for $5 or more. How much trade you attract will determine your overall income.

Hours

Choose whatever spare time you wish for the actual repair work, but someone should be home to accept the work brought in and estimate a price whenever customers come.

Requirements

You can learn the best materials for patching scarred wood and metal toys, and the sources for replacement parts from the distributors of the brand name toys. You'll have to ask. A few materials, paints, and tools also will be needed, and a work space in garage or basement.

Future

There are some toy clinics operating as full-time stores, and this is a clear possibility; but the best opportunity for expanding this sideline lies in acquiring discarded toys and restoring them for resale.

For Information

Write toy manufacturers (after obtaining their addresses from local distributors listed in your telephone book) and ask for booklets, brochures, catalogs, and any repair manuals or instructions they may have. Also inquire at hobby shops for repair materials, tools, and instruction booklets.

BABY-SITTING

If you have children and must stay home to take care of them, or if you just enjoy children and would like to profit by caring for and playing with them, baby-sitting can be an ideal job for you. Sometimes, of course, you can perform this service in other people's homes, but in the daytime, usually, mothers who work are willing to drop off their children and pick them up later.

Earnings

Limited. Usually a daytime rate would be about $.50 an hour, but if you care for half a dozen children at a time and make it your business to keep them all happy, well-fed, safe, and napped, you are thereby earning $3 an hour for as many hours as you wish.

Hours

You set your own, but the biggest demand is for sitters for the children of working mothers, meaning regular daytime work from about 8:00 A.M. to 5:00 P.M., in most cases.

Requirements

Tender loving care, watchfulness, and safe premises with perhaps a number of large or small toys to amuse children would be the only requirements; although you should check with your local Department of Welfare, which often requires registration for those who care for the children of others. It's a simple form.

Future

Many stay-at-homes have created their own day nursery school for large numbers of children, say, two dozen at a time, by developing a play program for them and by providing a number of small swings, toys, and books to amuse them. Others have boosted their income by providing such special services as pickup and delivery, or arranging to meet grade school children after the schoolday and taking them home until their mothers return from work to pick them up, solving a problem which has kept many would-be working mothers from being able to go to work.

For Information

Advertise for the work at your local supermarket bulletin board, in your local newspaper, on the bulletin board or in the employee paper at large nearby firms, or in your neighborhood churches.

BABY-SITTING VARIATIONS

Some people have made profitable their part-time hours at home by baby-sitting without ever caring for youngsters. When people are going away on vacation they need somebody to care for their plants and feed their pets, or just to watch their house and turn on the lights inside at night. And what about the goldfish and the lawn? If you wish to baby-sit without caring for children, advertise a sitter's service for everything for the family that's going away. Fees will be small and hinge on the work required, but some of the tasks are so simple that you could fill your den with goldfish bowls, sprinkle in a little food every morning, and that's it. People vacation for weeks at a time, so it all adds up, even at only $.50 a day. You must advertise for this work, and the likeliest spots, in addition to those listed above under baby-sitting, are luggage shops, travel bureaus, and automobile clubs.

PLATING AND CHROMING

You can create attractive, profitable articles out of your customer's souvenirs by offering a plating and chroming service for everything from jewelry to baby's shoes. In most cases, no expensive equipment or complicated know-how is required, since simple dip or spray processes are involved. There are many items that can be made and sold at higher prices with such plating, too. Simple engraving, an extra connected service could multiply your profits. Everyone wants to save baby's first shoes. If you contact the mothers through advertising, they bring the shoes to you. You plate them in chrome, bronze, copper, or whatever, at double the cost of your materials, plus the pay service charge, and then you add another charge for engraving on the toe of the plated shoe with the baby's name and perhaps the date she started walking.

Earnings

Usually people will pay $2 a pair for a plating job on baby shoes, because the souvenir means so much to them. If you get enough jobs, you can do a pair a day in an hour or less and reap $14 for very little effort per week.

Hours

You set your own; work when you feel like it.

Requirements

If you can follow simple instructions and purchase a few inexpensive supplies and tools, you can go into business. You must advertise; besides your local paper, try the children's shoe stores.

Future

Some large companies subsist on no other service than plating, dealing in a variety of industrial and retail products. So the extent to which you develop such a business will depend only on your own investment in time and money.

For Information

Write HBS Equipment Company, 3543 East 16th Street, Los Angeles, California. Box 943, Goleta, California. For engraving, try your local hobby shop or write to Engraving Division, Warner Electric, 1512 Jarvis, Chicago, Illinois 60626.

PACKAGING

Ever struggled with string and paper in a rush to get a gift or package properly prepared for the mails? Many people have, and if you can do a good job of it easily—it's a knack— then there are plenty of people who would rather have you do it, and they will pay you for the service. Sometimes you can offer a service such as this in connection with a large department store, with the firm paying you, or you can work from your home, with people bringing the things to you.

Earnings

Depending on whether you offer mailbox or post office delivery of the articles you wrap, you generally can charge $.50 to $1.50, plus postage, per package, and people will gladly pay it. The total income will be irregular, varying with how much work you are willing and able to attract.

Hours

If you're not at home when customers call, you lose a job, so this is good work for those who must stay home most of the time anyway. Busiest times usually will be the weekend shopping days and the gift days such as Christmas, Mother's Day, Father's Day, etc.

Requirements

Ability to bundle up an attractive package that meets all the demands of the postal system; the post office will be glad to tell you what these are for local and overseas mailing. You'll have to stock a small supply of various gift wrappings, ribbons, and heavy wrapping paper and string, and you'll need a small postal scale so you can compute postage before the customer leaves the article entirely in your hands. Any small table area in your house can be enough space to operate this business. You will have to advertise, either in stores or at the post office, in the latter case appealing to those who have just got off one bundle but would be glad to know next time that there's somebody to whom they can turn over the whole job.

Future

Particularly if you are located near a post office, or if there is such a store vacancy, a full-time packaging service could be offered. The operation could be supplemented by offering a variety of things for sale—greeting cards, gifts, other things to be packaged and mailed.

For Information

Contact your post office for its parcel mailing instructions.

CLEANUP

This is a job that spans a wide variety of tasks, from washing walls, to shampooing carpets and polishing floors. If you have a small pickup truck you could take jobs cleaning yards and garages and hauling the trash away, or you could specialize in wall washing, floor polishing, or complete housecleaning for working mothers. The work can be hard sometimes, but anyone can learn to do a good job, and if you build up regular customers you will have an excellent side income.

Earnings

Unless you know how much work is involved in each individual job, it's difficult for you to set a price in advance, but asking for $3.50 an hour plus supplies is fair, if the competition isn't asking less.

Hours

You set your own hours, at your convenience and the customer's; but usually when somebody calls, they will want the work done as soon as possible, so it's best to have a few hours available every day.

Requirements

Willingness to work and some basic equipment. If you do not wish to invest at first, such equipment as floor waxers and rug shampoo machines are available for rental when the job calls for them. You'll have to advertise your service in local newspapers, at apartment buildings, office buildings, and similar rental complexes.

Future

You can build up a complete janitorial route or make a full-time good living by serving a few entire office buildings with nightly floor care, dusting, and trash hauling, working with only a few basic tools to make it easier for yourself, and transportation.

For Information

This is a self-starting job you'll have to initiate yourself. Look in your local newspaper under services and compare prices. Then jump into the business yourself by placing your own similarly worded ad.

Chapter 5
A PRODUCT YOU CAN SELL

Among the most fortunate persons in the world today are those who have discovered the answer to their income problems in selling. Of all the tens of thousands of possible occupations that a man or woman can pursue, there are few that can equal selling for the fantastic benefits the seller gets, right from the start, whether working full time or part time, and whether or not he creates his own product of just pockets commissions on the sale of other's goods.

Think of it: how many jobs are there that you can start with little or no investment, be your own boss from the very first day, with no fear of being fired, and with complete confidence that your income will be limited only by your own efforts, not the whims of economic trends, factory contracts, or the dubious temper of a foreman? No wonder so many people who start out selling things in a small way to supplement their regular income end up quitting their jobs and becoming full-time salesmen, making more money with less effort than ever before in their lives. Salesmen are so much in demand that they'll never be out of work. Millions of jobs are open, even part time, and bosses are begging for men and women to fill these positions, offering them cars, expense accounts, commissions, and guarantees that assure their financial success.

Well, most people will ask at this point, if it's such a good job, how come there are so many vacancies? You know the answer. A lot of people are afraid to try selling. Personal rejection is a very delicate psychological matter and some people visualize all selling in terms of door-to-door canvassing, where they fear such crushing, discouraging blows as the slamming of doors in their faces. And, these same people will say, in selling you never know what you will earn; if you don't make any sales you don't make any money. They'd rather have $3 an hour, for sure, than $20 an hour, maybe. The answer to these complaints is that they are true; but you are making a big mistake if you think this way, because you are looking at the prospects completely negatively!

Think again. Every article you possess—your clothes, your furniture, the children's toys, the work-saving appliances in the kitchen, the drapes or pictures that decorate your walls, your automobile, books, newspapers, little luxuries—all of these were sold to you by someone who profited by the sale. Were you gruff or impolite with the salespeople who sold you these things? Of course not; such cases are rare, and they are rare because the things you bought were things you needed or wanted. In at least 80 per cent of the cases of all the purchases you made, you are the one, in fact, who initiated the sale by actually seeking out the salesman. If you went to a store seeking a television set and the salesman tried to interest you in a combination stereo, tape recorder, and television set, you probably said, "no," firmly, unless you were really interested. And that is the extent to which rejection should be weighed. A person who does not want, does not need, or cannot afford an article will not buy it, and that's all there is to it. Selling is mostly a matter of weeding out the no's and the yes's and you don't even need a thick skin to figure out that there's nothing personal in a complete stranger, or even a close friend, telling you, "No thanks, not today, anyway." Some very timid people who recognize this fact have turned out to be very good salesmen. In the rare cases where someone is rude to a salesman, chances are that something other than the salesman is bothering them. After all, selling is a business proposition, and common courtesy is generally observed unless one of the parties is out of wack. Maybe a salesman gets overly aggressive in his determination to display a product, or maybe a disinterested prospect has just had a fight with his wife or a bawling out by his boss.

Unpleasantness in selling is actually a rarity, and for good, sound reason. People enjoy buying things; they like to spend money. There is a sense of power in the selection of purchases, an enjoyment in acquiring the object you need, a gratification, and amid this feeling of good will, one usually reacts to salesmen with feelings of largess and gratuitousness, glad that the salesperson has been given the opportunity to benefit from a transaction which exchanges honest dollars for an article that is desired. This is the usual emotion involved in selling. Think about your own purchases and you will realize that this is true.

So much for the one big objection most people have to the idea of selling things for a living. You'll never know how easy selling can be until such negative notions are dismissed. If the article for sale is wanted, the customers come to you; if the article is much in demand and the price is a bargain, buyers will pound at your door with money in their hands. If you don't believe that's true, make a simple test. Look at your newspaper want ads in any merchandise category and price the articles. Now, if there was one ad there which offered comparable items for 20 per cent less, who would get all the calls?

A few years ago, the U.S. Department of Agriculture made a survey of selling tactics in men's clothing stores. In the case of men's suits, according to the survey findings, 839 out of 1,113 sales were made by salesmen who did nothing more than show the available merchandise to customers who walked in and asked for a suit. Without a word of encouragement or advice! Take it or leave it; buy or don't buy. But approximately 85 per cent of the customers bought suits because they wanted them. So selling is not difficult. Of course, with a little help to the potential customers, a little advice on materials, fittings, or values, the salesmen could have doubled their sales.

One truth about buying that every sales manager repeats again and again to his salesmen is this: "People don't buy what they need, or only reluctantly. They buy the things they want!" You can observe the difference by driving through the poorest section of any town. Even where food might be scarce on the table or clothing shabby, you will often see television aerials from the homes and shiny automobiles parked in the driveways. The trick of the salesman, in fact his only task, is to demonstrate or otherwise convince the prospect that the product would be desirable for him. Once the want, the emotion of desire, is created, the salesman won't be able to get away until the customer's wish is satisfied.

So how do you get started in this interesting and profitable field? Even if you have never sold a thing before, you can start because no experience is necessary—only the willingness to try and the ability to learn.

Naturally, if you are interested in rapidly putting dollars in your pocket you will choose small sales items, the purchase of which doesn't involve a lot of consideration on the part of the buyer. The decision-making process may mean a family budget conference and the delay of, "Come back next week after I've had a chance to talk to my wife," (or compare prices), or, "How about payday after next?" If you are selling pianos or encyclopedias with no low down payment plan, you might get this reaction. But if you are selling magazines and there is a story the customer wants to read, you have an immediate sale.

One thing you should be sure you do in selecting a product to sell is this: pick something which appeals to you personally. If you like a product and believe in its worth, if you believe it is a bargain and can save customers money, make them happy, healthy, safe, or save them work, or do some other pleasant service, then you will sell much more. Beginners usually do best with a product which sells itself, either because it is attractive or because advertising has already created widespread desire for the item. Such articles require only a brief sales pitch.

Don't worry about job-hunting. You don't have to file lengthy applications for salesmen's jobs and go through personal interviews that trace every job you ever had and what your marks were in algebra during the first year of high school. Companies will be eager to hear from you; in fact, they will woo you. And why shouldn't it be so? After all, you are willing to try to sell their product, and they will benefit along with you from your efforts.

Simply select an item you would like to sell, write to a firm which makes or distributes the product, and it will be glad to send you full information, sales kits, short courses on how it has been proven best to go about selling their product, and how much you will be able to earn for your efforts. They will practically take you by the hand and lead you to your first customer.

Before we get into listing possible profitable sales items for you, remember, the easiest selling of all is where the customers come to you. Advertising is the principal way of attracting people, whether you spend money for newspaper space, or just have a product so desirable that word of mouth brings new customers to you. When you go into selling on any scale, even on the basis of a few hours a week, to that extent you are an independent businessman. Reading about sales and customers in the final chapter of this book will prove beneficial and profitable.

Meanwhile, you will note that the job listings in this chapter have been simplified and do not follow the pattern set earlier. This is because in selling, several of the usual job variables, such as requirements, earnings, hours, and future prospects are very much the same whatever the product and it would be redundant to repeat the factors with each article.

A few of the points already have been mentioned. In almost all selling jobs, little or no investment is required other than a sales kit or original few items for display, and there is no barrier in terms of age, experience, or the hours you have available. All that is required is the willingness to sell. Your earnings and your hours are almost totally up to you. The income will depend on how much time you spend in selling, and how well you spend it. Commissions for selling are very liberal, so much so that even in the lowest echelon of selling, door-to-door canvassing, one sale an hour can make that hour well worth while, topping the hourly wage of employees working for someone else. The profits can be fantastic. Suppose you are selling aluminum siding for homes. You have a sales kit consisting of a briefcase with the material samples, the manufacturer's and the installer's guarantees, the prices and terms, and enough basic information to qualify your customer to see if they can afford your product. You don't have to go from one door to the next. Chances are, the company has already supplied you with a list of probable customers; or if not, you can tell by looking at the houses whether they need your product or could be made to want it. How? You tell them, and it is true: your house will be one of the best looking on the block. You'll never have to paint it again. Your insurance rates may be lowered. If you sold the house the day after the installation you'd get more than double your money back. One sale a week could make you from $100 to $1000, and most likely closer to $1000, depending on the size of the job. A $500 commission would be average for materials and labor that cost $1000. The job sells for, say, $1,950, so the company profits, too. Unbelievable? Ask a siding salesman. Of course, you and your company can sell more jobs if you lower your commissions and your prices, but these depend on several market conditions such as overhead, the plentifulness of financing money, and the number of sales prospects. The commission ratio remains high even when dealing in small sales. You can sell big, three-by-five foot display American flags for $1.95—a real bargain—and pocket half the sales price as your commission.

Another glorious aspect of being a salesman is that you can work pretty much at the time of day and the number of hours you wish. Do you only have Saturday afternoons available? That's sufficient time to show a good profit. Can you work only after dark? That's when most husbands are home from work and can make purchase decisions alongside their wives. Actually, if you learn to qualify prospects in advance, a few hours a week, at your own choosing and the convenience of customers, can be enough to make a big difference in your weekly income.

As for the future prospects of all selling jobs, in most cases the ceiling is unlimited. Women have started out making fancy candles in their home and selling them to friends, only to wind up renting a store and opening a candle shop because the profits were irresistible. From single sales it is easy to graduate to mass sales, and to make the customers come to you. There is hardly an item sold which could not turn out to be a wholly supporting venture. Millionaires have started out in door-to-door selling only to discover the magic key—something that people want and will be eager to pay for. Thus you build your income and enjoy a life of ease and prosperity, for the simple service of giving people the article they want and taking their money. You can develop into a distributor with your own salesmen, or a retail store owner, or a manufacturer. Thousands of people have done it.

If you enjoy meeting people, talking to them about yourself, and inquiring about their lives, chances are selling will be the most enjoyable job you've ever had. If not, there are ways you can be a salesman without ever knocking on a door, without ever accosting a stranger with a product in your hand. In fact, if you know how, without ever even meeting a customer face to face.

So read on, pick your product, examine its possibilities, and find the one you like best. Then let it work for you and pay all your bills. Let it put so much money in your pocket that you will be visiting other salesmen to buy the things *you* want!

SELL MATCHBOOK ADVERTISING

Businesses of all kinds—restaurants, gas stations, food stores, motels and dozens of others, practically every company listed in your Yellow Pages—are prospects for book match sales. This independent job requires no inventory and no investment. They are easy to sell because everybody likes to see his name in print, and there are continuing, no-effort reorders. Commissions vary, depending on the size of the order and style of printing, but you can make $60 in a half day's work. Write Superior Match Company, 7530 South Greenwood Avenue, Chicago, Illinois 60619; or Monarch Match Company, 2300 South First Street, San Jose, California 95150. They'll set you up in business.

SELLING PRINTING

You call on big and small business firms and show them an attractive portfolio of printing needs to meet their requirements for business cards, letterheads, envelopes and forms, take their orders, and mail them to the home office, which takes care of everything from there. You can make up to $100 a week in your spare time with just a couple of hours' work a day. For information and your own free business cards, write National Press, Department 960, North Chicago, Illinois 60064.

SELL COSMETICS

Women eagerly spend dollar after dollar on products which promise to make them more beautiful, so cosmetics are an easy item to sell, either door-to-door or through small, at-home parties which are fun as well as profitable. You start out with a handsome personal cosmetics kit of samples and take orders which give you a profit of up to 60 per cent of the sales price. For information write Studio Girl Cosmetics, 11461 Hart Street, North Hollywood, California 91605; Goodier Company, 400 North Bishop Avenue, Dallas, Texas 75208; Lucky Heart Cosmetics, 390 Mulberry Street, Memphis, Tennessee 38102; or look up your closest Avon distributor.

FASHION SALES CONSULTANT

Conduct fashion parties at home, inviting friends and their friends to a showing of lingerie, swimsuits, leisure wear, and other garments, and it all measures up to an average income of $50 a day. For information, write to Pennyrich International, 2613 Industrial Lane, Garland, Texas 75040; Hoover Manufacturing and Sales Company, 51-11 Queens Boulevard, Woodside, New York 11377; Frederick's, Inc., 6608 Hollywood Boulevard, Hollywood, California 90028; Fashion Frocks, 3301 Colerain, Cincinnati, Ohio 45225; or Beeline Fashions Company, 731 Fashion Plaza, Bensenville, Illinois 60106.

SELL CUSTOM UNIFORMS

Doctors, dentists, hospitals, restaurants, barber shops, and beauty salons are only a few of the customers who need uniforms for their entire staff. Working from a catalog and fabric samples, and promising swift delivery, you can earn more than $5 an hour taking orders for these much-in-demand garments. Write to Uniforms by Gilson, Inc., 2710 Hempstead Turnpike, Levittown, New York 11756.

SELL A VARIETY OF PRODUCTS

Multiplying your sales by variety, you can offer several different lines of products which women buy, all from the same company, including beauty aids, figure control garments, household products, nutritional food supplements, and fashions. For information contact Con-Stan Industries, 10912 Weaver Street, El Monte, California 91733.

SELL SHOES

Here is an item which makes every person you meet a potential customer, and you can display the merchandise by wearing a sample, showing off scores of other fashions in catalogs. Men or women. Several dollars profit for every small sale. For details, contact Charles Chester Shoe Manufacturing Company, Department 124, Brockton, Massachusetts 02403; Mason Shoe Manufacturing Company, Chippewa Falls, Wisconsin; or Bronson Shoe Company, 710 West Lake Street Minneapolis, Minnesota 55408.

SELL BRUSHES

The beauty of selling brushes, a variety of which are needed in every home, is that brush salesmen have traditionally become almost as welcome at every door as the mailman. Often it is a matter of passing out free catalogs and returning later to take the orders. Contact your area Fuller Brush Company distributor listed in your telephone book, or write Superb Brush Company, Inc., East Greenville, Pennsylvania 18041.

SELL PROFIT TO OTHERS

That's right! Here is a specialty which involves the biggest replacement item in a women's wardrobe, yet requires no door-to-door sales. The idea is that in every community there are women's clubs, school groups, church organizations, and dozens of other units eager to raise funds for their causes. You sell them a hosiery-sales plan that will bring stockings to women at below retail costs, earn money for their organizations, and earn profit for yourself. Everybody benefits. No inventory, no bookkeeping, and no collections for you. For information on plan write Genie Limited, 3912 Campus Drive, Newport Beach, California 92660.

SELL MAGAZINES

Almost every home uses at least one magazine regularly, and people know they can save by subscribing. Selling magazines can be as easy as establishing the fact that you have the subscriptions to sell. This can be done by telephone, advertising, or just passing the word around among friends. Your profit is usually from 30 to

60 per cent of the subscription price, and the renewals are easy! Contact International Circulation Distributors, 250 West 55th Street, New York, New York 10019; Qualified Reader's Service, Box 151, Woodmere, New York, 11598; or check the magazine distributorships in the Yellow Pages of your local telelphone directory.

BOOKS AND ENCYCLOPEDIAS

If you are selling a major item like an encyclopedia or set of books, all you need is one sale a week or one a month to make it profitable. Some people find them easy to sell, particularly to families who feel the product is necessary to their children's education. Usually you talk to people and make appointments with them—or the appointments are made for you!—because the purchase is a family decision. A prestige product. Contact Encyclopedia Americana, Putnam Valley, New York, New York, 10579, or Encyclopedia Britannica, 425 North Michigan Avenue, Chicago, Illinois 60601.

SELL INSURANCE

Many part-time opportunities exist in this profitable occupation which puts money in your pocket every time there is a policy renewal. Just passing out insurance pamphlets door to door, talking to your friends, or simply making appointments for an experienced broker can be very profitable. Many local agencies will be willing to teach you and often supply you with a car for your calls. It is satisfying work because you are helping people with lifetime security. Contact local insurance agencies directly.

SELL JEWELRY

Nothing sells itself as quickly as jewelry, which you can wear and show around, taking orders from your friends and contacts for gifts or for themselves. Commissions range from 60 to 200 per cent on a single item, and customers send more business to you. For information and catalogs, write to Charm and Treasure, Inc., 1201 Avenue of the Americas, New York, New York 10036; or Jakla Gem Company, Box 20044, St. Petersburg, Florida 33702.

SELL MAILBOX AND HOUSE NUMBERS

This is a specialty that is best done from door to door in the daytime. You ask homeowners if they want their house numbers on their mailboxes, curbstones, or doorposts, and it is a service-sale that every home needs for identification to friends and especially for deliveries and emergencies. The usual charge is $1 and the job requires a small investment in a stencil kit available at most hardware and stationery supply shops. Check your Yellow Pages under Stencils.

SELL AUTOMOBILE ADVERTISING SIGNS

Every businessman knows the value of advertising, and if he is overlooking his company vehicles, he will be eager to buy doorside or rear signs which are affixed to the vehicles, displaying his company name and service or product, plus telephone number. Larger companies will buy dozens at a time. Commissions of 50 per cent and more. For information and sales kits, contact Wayde Smith Company, 1465½ Firestone Boulevard, La Mirada, California; Keyser Plastics, Inc., 1148 Capouse Avenue, Scranton, Pennsylvania 18509; or Pirad Plastics, 1466 Callens Road, Ventura, California 93003.

SELL ADVERTISING SPECIALTIES

Other salesmen and all the business firms in town are prospects for such items as calendars, which many firms would like to distribute once a year—if they thought to order them in time. Also popular in large quantities are give-away ball-point pens with advertising on them. Salesmen call them door-openers. Colorful advertising calendars can be bought by you for $8.25 a hundred, pens at one hundred for $11, for high profit resale. Many other items. For sales kit contact National Press, Department 912, North Chicago, Illinois 60064.

SELL ALBUMS FOR PHOTOS

Every home treasures its family snapshots and is always in the market for a bigger, better album. An ideal gift item too. Profits range from 50 to 100 per cent on retail prices $5.95 to $15.95. Give photographers a commission and let them sell them for you! Contact Hometown Album Plan, 2321 Santa Clara Avenue, Alameda, California.

SELL LABELS

Have you ever seen ads offering 1,000 gummed labels with any name, address, and zip code for $1 and wondered how they could possibly sell at such a bargain price? Insiders know that there is well over 200 per cent profit on each sale! You can take orders for the labels from your friends and from businesses for $1 or more and your cost per 1,000 is only $.35. For every 10,000, that makes $6.50 profit, and if you advertise, orders can come in at the rate of a dozen or more a day. No printing or even delivery work for you; company does it all. Write Brewster Sales, 808 Washington Street, St. Louis, Missouri 63101.

SELL MUTUAL FUNDS

One of the hottest investments of the modern day, mutual funds are combined stock market portfolio ventures that practically take all the risk out of the stock market. And most of the mutual fund companies have investment plans which allow a person to put a little money every month or whenever he can afford, after an initial payment which goes mostly to the salesman! We are talking about hundreds of dollars per sale and a prestige profession that has the satisfaction of helping other people make money. As you gain experience in this field, you may find your eyes opened to inside stock market information that could make you rich from your own investments. Contact local offices of the mutual funds which advertise in the financial pages of your closest large city newspaper or write Career Academy's Division of Investment Banking, 825 North Jefferson Street, Milwaukee, Wisconsin, for home study course.

SELL LIFETIME METAL SOCIAL SECURITY PLATES

Everybody carries a Social Security card and losing it or having it defaced can cause troublesome and costly red tape for replacement. So everyone is a prospect for a permanent metal card. Big profits for multiple sales. For free samples and sales kit write Russell, Box 286, Pulaski, Tennessee 38478; or Perpetual Perma Products, Box 1913D, Meridian, Mississippi 39301.

SELL HOLIDAYS

Dream vacations for two in Miami or Las Vegas, and other alluring tourist spots, are offered by many merchants as prizes to attract customers in throngs. Every wholesale or retail merchant will recognize the value of this deal and the seller earns a big 40 per cent commission. Write Exclusive Holidays, Inc., 1911 North East 168th Street, North Miami Beach, Florida; or Tango, 6611 Allen Street, Hollywood, Florida.

SELL TOYS AND NOVELTIES

Small attractive items sell on impulse either directly to your friends or by the dozens to small merchants. Or you can set up your own display racks for retail sales, or advertise the products and sell in large quantities. You buy for pennies, sell at double the price to wholesale outlets, or at triple to five times the cost at retail. You can concentrate on a few of the hundreds of items available, displaying samples of them. Or offer hundreds of them from catalogs. For information write Specialty Merchandise Corporation, 7630 Gloria Avenue, Van Nuys, California 91406; or Worldwide Bargainhunters, Box 730, Holland, Michigan 49423.

SELL MEN'S ACCESSORIES

Men look at and quickly buy sales kit items like attractive belt buckles, tie clasps, money clips, cuff links and pins. Mass sales opportunities, too, form occupational lapel identification badges, other articles. For information and sales kit contact Hook-Fast, Box 1088, Providence, Rhode Island.

SELL IMPORTED WARES

Bargains from across the borders and over the seas are always appealing to buyers because the articles for sale are different and people know that low foreign labor costs mean bargain prices and extra quality in hand-made goods. Catalogs and sales samples available: Mexico Imports, Lumbley, Post Office Box 5535, San Diego, California 92105; or International Buyers, Box 4633, Colorado Springs, Colorado 80909.

SELL HOMES

If you really want to sell for big money, sell big products, like homes, where your commission, usually on a percentage of the total sale price, can run into hundreds of dollars from a single sale. Most states require real estate sales people to be licensed, but do permit trainees or part-time workers to canvass for business, which simply means asking people if they want to sell their homes. The broker does the paper work, paying you for the listing. You usually can sell bargain, pre-cut homes for a manufacturer, however, without training for a real estate license, and this, too, can be a profitable occupation full or part time. For information on pre-cut homes sales write Franklin Thrift Homes, 1600 North Atherton Street, State College, Pennsylvania. Or, for jobs canvassing for listings you can telephone an inquiry to local real estate agents. For home training course write: Weaver School of Real Estate, 3521 Broadway, Kansas City, Missouri 64111.

SELL CHARM

Here is a commodity you have to have a little of to sell a lot of— a home study course in charm. You can operate a profitable sales and service line from your own home or through the mails. Your own cost is as low as $35 per course, while the company finances costs of customers up to $395 per course, so the big profits are obvious. Rental plans, too. For information on charm course sales contact Royce Publishing, Box 204, Dolton, Illinois 60419.

SELL HISTORICAL REPRODUCTIONS

Schools, banks, and other prestige institutions are markets for big sales of historical reproductions of authentic old newspapers, maps, documents, and posters for advertising and educational purposes. Just showing samples around is often all it takes to sell large quantity orders. Terrific for historic birthday sales promotions or Americanism campaigns. Contact Hilltop Enterprises, 65 East I, Chula Vista, California 92010; or Garens, Box 517, Xenia, Ohio 45385.

SELL SPORTING GOODS

Fishing and camping are among the biggest, fastest growing fields today among leisure industries. Particularly if you are located in or around an area where fishing, hunting, and camping are regional attractions, this could be the sales market for you. Locating the camping enthusiasts is all it takes to make the sales in plentiful volume. For information write H. C. Buicke & Sons, 90 Stark Street, Tonawanda, New York 14150.

SELL WIGS, WIGLETS, AND FALLS

Hair is a gold mine today, a product that was barely on the market a few years ago. You can sell your own exclusive line of wigs and falls from your own home or by spreading the word around women's clubs or schoolgirls. A big inventory isn't necessary; you can sell from small samples and catalogs, promising hair color matching on a custom basis. For information write Fashion Associates, Inc., 418 Armour Circle, North East, Atlanta, Georgia 30324, or Miller-Rogers, Inc., 410 Beach Boulevard, Hallandale, Florida 33009.

SELL OIL PORTRAITS FROM PHOTOS

Everybody has a favorite photo and from one sample oil painting taken from a photo, you can sell dozens in a profitable, easy occupation. For details write Boston Oil Portrait Company, Suite 34, 74 The Fenway, Boston, Massachusetts 02115.

SELL FURNITURE

This is a highly competitive field which often requires big inventories and big investments, but there are several ways to eliminate these handicaps and reap the very attractive markup that makes furniture sales a crowded field. If you are reasonably handy, you can shop for slightly damaged freight goods—objects like coffee tables, chairs and desks, bureaus with broken legs or chipped drawers—replace the damaged legs or restore the broken piece, and sell the item as good as new. The same can be done by buying used pieces of furniture and refinishing them, or dressing up unfinished furniture with, for example, mar-proof plastic finish and more attractive drawer pulls. Or, furniture can be sold for approximately 50 per cent commission through catalogs which require no inventory at all. In most of the cases, small ads in the furniture listings, want ad section of your local newspapers, will bring bargain-hunters to your home; or write Fine State Furniture Guild, Post Office Box 5515, Winston-Salem, North Carolina 27101.

SELL FIRE EXTINGUISHERS

Here is a product that every home owner or car owner will immediately recognize the need for, and the seller gets the big plus satisfaction of knowing he is possibly saving lives as he earns his income. Small fire extinguishers, retailing from under $5 to about $12, produce commissions ranging from 40 to 60 per cent. For information write Merlite, 114 East 32nd Street, New York, New York 10016; or Hudson Manufacturing Company, Sheridan, Michigan.

SELL BEDSPREADS AND LINENS

These household necessities sell themselves if you display them in your home and show them to your friends, especially with the new popularity of king-size and queen-size beds making so many old bedspreads obsolete. Check your own local Yellow Pages for a wholesaler to supply you on small orders or write Old Colony Mills, Post Office Box 1442, Dalton, Georgia 30720.

SELL GREETING CARDS

Contrary to what many people think, greeting cards are not a seasonal business, even though sales skyrocket every Christmastime. There are so many birthdays, anniversaries, graduations, illnesses, and similar occasions which call for a greeting card that every home can use an assortment, and the humorous-type cards have got people sending each other greetings for no reason at all, other than to share a smile. Again, check your local Yellow Pages for a local wholesaler or write Carlton Card Company, 581 Fourteenth Street, Oakland, California; Hedenkamp & Company, 361 Broadway, New York, New York 10013; or Creative Card Company, 4401 West Cermak Road, Chicago, Illinois 60623.

SELL DOORMATS

Here is one example of a small specialty that can let you make yourself welcome at every door in town. Take orders for rubber doormats bearing the customer's own name—a hard-to-find article. And you don't even have to carry them in stock. Contact Mitchell Division, Royal Industries, 1500 East Chestnut Street, Santa Ana, California 92701.

SELL HOUSEWARES

Easy to sell by demonstrating them in your own home at invite-a-friend parties, which are becoming popular fun all over the country. No investment, no deliveries, and no collecting necessary. For information write House of Plastic, Avon, Connecticut 06001. Ask also about their extra toys and gifts for seasonal profits.

SELL AUTO SEAT COVERS

Print a business card with your telephone number, find a seat cover maker who'll give you a low price for the benefit of your business, then go around parking lots and curbsides, wherever autos are lined up, and pick out the ones which need new seat upholstery. Write on your cards, "I can get you seat covers for this car for $14.98," or whatever price you can profitably sell at, and watch the business pour in; it's the personal touch that does it, and your only investment is business cards.

BE AN AGENT

If your regular work brings you in contact with a lot of people or homes, or if it could, then you may be overlooking a big chance for the easiest commissions in the world. Visit retailers who deal in, for example, draperies, carpets, painting, roofing, auto body repairs, or aluminum screens, and offer to sell for them, strictly on outside sales, if they'll print up business cards for you. Whenever you meet someone who mentions needing a product or service, or when you see homes or businesses in obvious need, scribble a little personal message like, "Tell Jim I said he'd give you a good deal," and leave your card. The cards cost you nothing and the dealers usually are glad to pay a good commission on all business you bring in. Browse through your local Yellow Pages.

SELL ANYTHING AND EVERYTHING

Specific sales opportunities listed so far are only a random sampling of the thousands of possibilities awaiting you. No one book could describe them all. The sales category in want ads throughout the country generally is the biggest part of the help needed listings. Sell doors, franchises, packaged meats to markets, frozen foods, paper products, film and visual aids, liquor, metal and other raw materials, music and record albums, hair improvement and barber supplies, lighting, bricks and home building materials, club memberships, medical equipment and drug supplies, business machines, water softening, transportation, computer services, engineering, vehicle rentals, education, or a score of other services. You don't have to sell tangible products and, of course, you can sell products or services at the wholesale, retail, or manufacturing level. For general and specific ideas on products and sales, subscribe to the monthly magazine, Salesman's Opportunity, for $5. Write the magazine subscription department at John Hancock Center, Suite 1460, 875 North Michigan Avenue, Chicago, Illinois 60611. If you are interested in selling, but need to bolster your confidence or improve your ability, write for a free aptitude test from Sales Training Institute, 1650 Wilshire Boulevard, Los Angeles, California 90017.

MAIL ORDER SALES

Multiplying sales possibilities a thousand-fold, use of the U.S. government's marvelous and inexpensive postal system can bring your fortune to your mailbox, and there is hardly a product or service imaginable that can't be sold by mail. With this kind of selling, you never see your customers, and you don't even have to stock, own, or invest in the products you sell! Most mail order sales employ a principle called drop-shipping. It works like this: From a general merchandise company, or one dealing in a specific line of products, you obtain a catalog listing the items they sell and their prices and markups. You advertise these products in magazines or by direct mail, stamping your own name on brochures or catalogues, and when the orders come in, you send them on to the company involved. They ship the desired article direct to the buyer and you collect a commission on every sale, the difference between the wholesale and retail price. In the mails you are dealing with mass sales, even on a regional or local basis, so the profit per item doesn't have to be big. Ten cents profit per item on a new and unusual can opener, for example, adds up to $100 when you sell 1,000, and the markups usually are much higher. Ideas are the key to riches in this branch of sales, and many persons have made huge fortunes through the mails by finding a product that appeals to the public and offering it to them through advertising, whether in magazines, newspapers, or direct mail. There are millions of homes in the country, and therefore unlimited prospects, but you don't have to contact every one of them in your efforts. A product aimed at new mothers, newlyweds, graduates, used car owners, music lovers, or any special category, can be sold directly to these likely prospects by procuring a mailing list of such selected categories; see your Yellow Pages under mailing lists for such lists. Even if you do not go into mail order sales nationally or dealing with big merchandise firms, you can work locally with big profits.

Suppose you look around at small specialty or variety stores in one section of town. Chances are the retailer's entire profit, or 90 per cent of it, comes from customers in his immediate neighborhood or section of town. Maybe the retailer has one very attractive article for sale that is not available elsewhere, or is better made or cheaper than others like it. You can see the retail prices of his merchandise. Ask him what it would be worth to him if you could sell a hundred of them a week, more than he is now selling. He may already have sales brochures on the item or items, or perhaps can get them from the manufacturer. You offer to send them to all the homes in other parts of town, or advertise in papers there, soliciting mail orders. The extra sales are going to cost him nothing but a commission for you, so he has nothing to lose. He may even set you up with a desk and pay postage, too! Keep your eyes open for this kind of opportunity. There are numerous firms which offer to show you step-by-step all the details and opportunities of mail order sales, and you may write them for specifics. A few are: Mellinger, Inc., 1554 South Sepulveda Boulevard, Los Angeles, California 90025; Vikari's, Post Office Box 1312, Salt Lake City, Utah 84110; or Quest Enterprises, Post Office Box 6029, San Jose, California 95150.

Most of the sales opportunities outlined above lend themselves to mail order sales as well as direct-contact sales. In addition, there are a number of products which you can make yourself and sell, profiting both on the manufacture and the sales! And mail order applies to these opportunities as well. Keep your imagination working: here are many possibilities to provide food for thought:

MAKE PLASTIC NOVELTIES

In your own home, you can start a little factory that turns out as many as fifty different items in plastics—toys, dolls, animals, guns, wall plaques and even Christmas decorations—with no special skills or previous experience. Produce $100 worth of retail merchandise a day, for sale to merchants, mail orders, or your own home store. An investment in plastic vacuum mold equipment and raw materials is required. For free samples and information write Nationwide Plastics Company, 12305 Hawthorne Boulevard, California 90250.

MAKE CANDLES

Colorful, specially decorated candles for year-round display and big holiday demand. It's a fascinating hobby for some people, and it can be a profitable part-time job molding and decorating them. Ask a gift shop to sell them for you on consignment or deliver them to stores by the dozens for wholesaler's profits. Facts and instructions from Candle Institute, 1600 Cabrillo Avenue, Torrance, California 90501.

WOODWORKING

For the man with his own home jigsaw, skillsaw, or other hobby tools, there are dozens of profitable projects—shelves, novelties, utility racks, etc. Make one or a dozen items; show them off to friends, or offer them to a small retailer for resale. For patterns and information write Constantine, 2051 Eastchester Road, Bronx, New York 10461; or Service Bureau, Popular Mechanics, 575 Lexington Avenue, New York, New York 10022.

MAKE CUSTOM CASES

Customers come to you and order them in advance for their own special use. All materials, instructions supplied. A little salesmanship is needed, but company tells you how to promote business. A little skill with tools required. Write Custom Case Supply Company, 7630 Gloria Avenue, Van Nuys, California 91406.

DO NEEDLECRAFT

Women who are handy with a needle and can do simple work sitting down in their spare time can turn out a variety of products, custom-made for customers, after turning out a few samples to show around. Patterns and easy-to-follow instructions for sewing, crocheting, knitting, creweling, weaving, embroidering, and tatting. Six-month subscription, $1, from Stitch 'n Sew, Post Office Box 412, Danvers, Massachusetts.

DO CONCRETE COLORING

Everywhere there is a concrete patio, driveway, stairs, or wall, there is an opportunity for turning the dull, concrete surface into a colorful thing of beauty with a long-lasting, penetrating stain that eats into the pores of the concrete and can't peel or wear off like paint. Test in your own yard and sell applications to your friends when they see the transformation. Or you can just sell the product itself at $12.95 a gallon, for a profit of $4.50 per gallon. Concrete cleaner also available. For information, write Beauty Stain Products Company, 3525 West Peterson Avenue, Chicago, Illinois 60645.

SELL CUSTOM SIGNS

From your own home shop you can turn out artistic, custom signs that look like you've been doing it for years. Every company needs its name on at least one sign, and there are dozens of common ones, like OPEN, CLOSED, FOR SALE, and even, CUSTOM SIGNS SOLD HERE. For information, write Tettaton, 1924 Salisbury, St. Louis, Missouri; Ben Kerns, Box 812, Greenville, South Carolina 29601; or Straley, 410 South Western, Springfield, Ohio 44506.

DO MARBLEIZING

Now liquid marble can be brushed, sprayed, or troweled onto any surface, or poured into molds, producing a slick, glazed, marble effect on concrete, wood, wallboard, iron, stone, or almost any other surface. This beautification process is much in demand today for custom tabletops, counters, walkways, statuary, and novelties. You make the products themselves or offer the application service. National Potteries Company, Grand Rapids, Minnesota.

DO LEATHERCRAFT

In your spare time you can pursue a creative, money-making hobby producing dozens of leathercraft items like belts, purses, handbags, wallets. Leather fashions have become one of the biggest sellers in recent seasons and the high prices haven't slowed down the trend. Hundreds of make-it ideas available in leathercraft catalog. Write Tandy Leather Company, Department M-67, Forth Worth, Texas.

SELL CHEMICALS AND SUPPLIES

This is a mass supply business that requires only the mixing and repackaging of materials in smaller quantities than you purchase wholesale. Resell to janitors, office buildings, hotels and motels, schools, and even homes. Did you know that one ideal, all-purpose cleaning compound that beats practically anything on the market for removing all dirt from glass, tile, painted surfaces, floors and woodwork is available at $.50 a gallon to the customer, at a 300 per cent profit for the wholesaler? Free details on a full line of chemicals and sanitation supplies from Surety Laboratories, 20 American Industrial Drive, Maryland Heights, Missouri 63042.

SELL REMNANTS

For quilt makers, pillow coverers, and just plain imaginative decorators, remnants are always in demand. For less than $10 you can buy them by the dozens of pounds, mix them up, and retail them to sewing clubs, your friends, or customers attracted by want ads in your newspapers, or cards placed on supermarket bulletin boards. Or you can take the material and turn it into profitable items yourself for a 200 to 300 per cent profit. For information and prices, write Helfand and Sons, 615 West Pershing Road, Chicago, Illinois 60609. Or National Cotton Council, Box 9906, Memphis, Tennessee 38112.

BE A DOLL MAKER

Some people do this as a satisfying hobby, but it can be a profitable occupation as well. Count on big seasonal sales at Christmastime, when a small ad or display in a variety store will sell them like hotcakes. If you come up with a specialty like foreign-dressed dolls, or a souvenir item like Indian dolls, miner dolls, or some other special dress that suits your region of the country, you can sell them by the dozens the year-round. Look what happened to Barbie Doll! Repairs and doll clothes can make money, too. Write Doll Hospital School, 2251 Barry Avenue, Los Angeles, California 90064.

CREATE VELVET

In this luxury market, the velvet look is considered the ultimate, and when you can sell it at a bargain, you have the opportunity to clean up. A new process utilizing a patented, portable electronic machine creates a velvet-like surface for walls, car tops, and furniture. An investment is required, but the manufacturer promises profits of $100 an hour from machine operation, which is an excellent return. For information write Velvet Marketing Division, Post Office Box 2397, Van Nuys, California 91404.

INSTALL UNDERGROUND SPRINKLERS

This can be a gold mine in the spring and summer, especially. Install sprinkler systems that automatically water the lawns of homes, apartment complexes, and institutions. Anyone who has seen one work and checked the low prices quickly realizes that there is a saving of hundreds of future hours' work hose watering by installing corrosion-proof, freeze-free plastic piping with pop-up sprinkler heads under lawns and along planted areas. Saves lawns and plants by making it so easy to water that they're never neglected. Depending on size of installation, you can charge a minimum of $5 an hour over and above material costs, and you profit on material costs, by buying at contractor prices. Contact local building supply or gardening shops for installation instructions and prices. Put one in at your own house for demonstration purposes and it'll pay for itself. Or write Rain Rite Products, 5960 Tension Drive, Fort Worth, Texas 76112.

BAKE CAKES

If you have a talent for baking cakes for your own family, why not advertise that you'll bake them for birthday parties and other occasions? Repeat orders and a reputation will keep things cooking.

MAKING MUSIC

Guitar and banjo-making kits can put you in business with a prestige, popular product that can be sold through music stores, personal demonstration, or local advertising. For information write Satinwood, 510 East 11th Street, New York, New York 10009.

MAKE YOUR OWN GALLERY

Whether this simple, easy-to-run sideline is more product or more service will depend on you, but there is money to be made for good causes and a chance to help deserving artists, even if you don't paint yourself. If you have a suitable room in your home or know of a banquet room or other high-traffic location where artwork could be hung, you can solicit local artists for the best of their works to display for sale. You make a percentage. If you organize a good representation of local talent, chances are there will be plenty of locations eager to have the exhibition—that is, if you don't have the room yourself. As a sideline you can offer framing services to the artists, which can help sell their work. Or frame and sell interesting prints which can be bought in variety from a large city bookstore nearby. Or write for old woodcut and engraving prints to Decorative Reproductions, Box 11321, Wichita, Kansas 67202.

MAKE CORSAGES

You can learn to grow your own orchids at home by creating the required conditions for this delicate and valuable flower. Sell them as is or offer them in corsages at prices up to $10 each. Or grow a variety of flower plants at home in pots for resale to florists or directly to customers. Place your card on hospital bulletin boards where they post visiting hours, and advertise ahead of Mother's Day and Easter. For ordinary flowers like carnations, start from seeds or bulbs, or write World of Orchids, 1356 Flower Street, Los Angeles, California 90015.

SELL BONSAI TREES

Miniature trees trained to grow to specially beautiful proportions, via an ancient Japanese art, are attractive plants that sells on sight to garden lovers for indoor or outdoor use. A rarity not available in many locales. Stores will buy them too, because suppliers are few and far between. For information, write United Miniature Tree Associates, 2933 Whittier Boulevard, Los Angeles, California 90023.

WORK VENDING MACHINES

This is not something you sell, but a whole different way of selling, and one of the easiest. Marketing through machines has been applied to almost every product from apples to zodiac forecasts. Any small items that people need can be suited to the simple process whereby customers deposit coins, press a button, and receive the desired object. Candy, coffee, postage stamps, trinkets, toiletries, music, fun and games, writing implements, and dozens of other hot sales articles adapt to these quick sales. You load the machines, walk away, and come back in a few days or a week to check on sales, replenish the stock, and pick up the money. Investment in the machines is required, of course, but once you've got them, and have built up your array of equipment, they work night and day for you. Use your imagination to figure out the best locations for various machines—combs in restrooms, postage stamps near the corner mailbox in a variety store, coffee, candy, and cigarette machines in high-traffic locations or places where people might have to be waiting. For an example of the outlay required, let's take ball—point pens, which sell very quickly near schools and in shopping centers. For an investment of $100, you get three $.25 ball–point pen vendors and 600 pens, which bring in an initial gross take of $150. There is a 25 per cent commission usually paid to locations to induce them to let you place your mechanical salesman in their store or on their premises, which in our example comes to $37.50, and the merchandise cost actually computes at $30. Your net profit on the deal, the first round of sales, is $82.50, meaning that after the first refill you have paid off your machine and are making a clear profit of 75 per cent, less merchandise at wholesale. For information write Parkway, 701-733 Ensor Street, Baltimore, Maryland 21202.

Chapter 6
PUTTING HOBBIES AND SPECIAL TALENTS TO WORK

Many people, when casting about looking for part-time work, overlook the fact that making money can be fun, and that something they like to do, and do very well, can bring in all the extra income they need: it is called a hobby.

Do you like to write things—just for yourself, you say—or do you paint or make flower arrangements? Do you love antiques? Maybe music or dancing is your greatest pastime. All of these hobbies, special talents, and interests and many more can be put to work for you in ways which will bring in a handy side income, and chances are you'll enjoy the pursuit more than ever before, because you'll be doing more of it and have the reward of money in your pocket in exchange for your pleasurable efforts.

Hobbies themselves have become such big business that stores all over the country are popping up to supply, serve, and profit from them, and if you think there is some special creative work that you would enjoy, investigate these shops and examine how easy it would be to make beautiful things, learning by the step-by-step instructions available. Most people do their best work when it's something they enjoy doing, so the combination of hobby and work usually is a happy one.

Most of the hobbies and special talents that adapt to quick profits can de done either in your own leisure hours at home or on a regular schedule for someone else, with a guaranteed income, which is another big attraction of jobs connected with the creative arts. And, in many cases, the sky is the limit when it comes to harnessing the profit possibilities of such work. Be realistic, though. Dreaming of a million dollar check for writing next year's biggest best-selling novel isn't going to solve today's money problems any more than dreaming of winning your local gas station lottery contest without buying any gas. If you recognize that investing time in your talents for profit might just be a long-shot, keep pursuing it as a hobby and look elsewhere for reliable profits. Or better yet, seek and find a job working for someone else, with a dependable hourly wage, for doing work that is connected with your special talents.

The following job opportunities should stimulate your thinking about turning fun into profit. Look at them all in relation to your own special likes and dislikes. If you wish to browse further into possible specialties, try the new magazine called "Hobbies With a Profit," (two sample copies for $1) by writing to Post Office Box 337, Seabrook, New Hampshire 03874.

BE A PHOTOGRAPHER

Anyone who can learn to operate a camera can make money from this fascinating pursuit, and the better your pictures, the higher the income. Even the simplest, inexpensive equipment, used in the right place at the right time, can produce a good spare-time income. Here are a few ideas: newborn babies' pictures at local hospitals are sure sellers, and generally the nursery department will take them for you because of hospital regulations and because they know parents want this service. You present proofs as quickly as possible and finished pictures by the time baby and mother leave the hospital. Summer camps are another ideal territory for quick snapshots, perhaps of the Polaroid type, because children attending seldom have a camera on hand to record their activities for their parents. You take the snapshots during the busy days, sell them to parents on visiting days or by mail. Animal shows are a much neglected opportunity—small horse shows, dog shows, cat shows, cattle shows—because usually the winners get photographed while the also-rans, whose owners are equally proud of them, are bypassed. There are dozens of losers for every winner. Stores and businesses are another inviting field of photo prospects. Most store owners are very proud of their businesses, and industry operators with their special machinery feel the same way; they could use pictures for their own satisfaction and for use in advertisements and small trade journals. Weddings are another rich prospect for candid photos, but you better know enough about cameras to not miss, or your first wedding job will be the last.

Some photographers operate a studio in their own homes, even with a minimum of skill, confining their business to fixed focus passport and identification photos. Polaroid owners can roam a beach where boys and girls together would love to have their picture taken, and see it right away. Home photographs also are good sellers; it's amazing that the vast majority of homeowners, even though they own a camera, never take a picture of their own house. If you can make the home look good, pride will sell the picture. There are dozens of photo sales ideas. Use your imagination.

Earnings

You can sell small pictures of people, animals, or things for $1 each, if you are on the spot with prints, instant Polaroid or regular film. Enlargements and extra copies can enlarge your profits, especially if you do your own processing. If you have a special talent with pictures, or if you can manage to be in the right place at the right time, you can sell them to people and publishers for $5, $50, $100, and even $500, each!

Hours

Swing your camera around your neck and go off on a profitable picture taking outing any time there is enough light and enough prospects. Unless you are shooting flash group photos or a special lighting assignment, you'll be able to work only daytime.

Requirements

All you need is a camera, the ability to operate it, and a field of prospects. Imagination will not only serve in producing better pictures, but will be needed for the ideas that turn a fun pastime into a profitable one.

Future

You can develop this art into a profitable, full-time studio operation or accept interesting travel assignments as a free-lance photographer for magazines. One twenty-seven-year-old free-lancer, among the best in the country, made $55,000 last year for his pictures!

For Information

Write New York Institute of Photography, 10 West 33rd Street, New York, New York 10001.

BE AN ARTIST

If you have art talent, you can have fun painting and make money selling your paintings at the same time. Several learn-by-mail schools offer a thorough training course to help you develop your art talent. You can then sell your paintings at local art exhibitions, by arranging to display them in local stores or restaurants, or by setting up your easel and doing portraits at shopping centers or recreation areas. (A commission or rental fee is generally required.)

Earnings

You can usually get between $5 and $15 for a portrait, depending on its size. An oil painting, such as a landscape, a clown, a kitten, or other favorites, can bring you between $25 or $100, depending on its size and, let's admit it, how good a painter you are. Don't forget to figure on the cost of material.

Hours

Paint 'em on weekday evenings, sell 'em on Saturdays. That's the usual formula, but again you can set your own hours.

Requirements

This one has a big requirement, which makes it unsuitable for most people: you've got to have art talent. If you thing you do, but you're not sure, you can take an art talent test by writing Famous Artists.

For Information

Write Famous Artists Schools, Westport, Connecticut 06880. Or Washington School of Art, Port Washington, Long Island, New York.

WRITE FOR MONEY

Anyone can write, and you don't have to pen a 200,000-word best-selling novel to make money writing. One writing coach who teaches people to profit from small paragraphs likes to cite the fact that the biggest-paid writer of the modern era wasn't Hemingway, but a suburban Chicago housewife who scribbled about a page of words and ended up with over $100 a word for it, from a national company that wanted to promote its products. If you can jot a two-line jingle of ten words and sell it for $5, you're earning $.50 a word, and many big-time professional writers would love to work for that rate! If you buy a Writers Market Yearbook for $7, you'll find thousands of markets for brief articles, from single paragraphs to 500-word stories, and if you learn to use it, you're in a profit-making business. As a writer you can turn out short articles on a free-lance basis from your home, or you can work part-time for a newspaper, magazine, advertising agency, public relations firm, or other publishers.

Earnings

Writing represents probably the most irregular of all occupations when it comes to free-lancing from your home. Checks that come in can range from $5 to $5,000. If you work for an employer, by the job or by the hour, the income is, of course, more regular, generally ranging from $3 to $10 an hour.

Hours

The beauty of this occupation is that you can work anywhere, anytime, as you wish. An idea that comes to you while driving to work at another job, and put into words that night at home on the kitchen table, can earn you $25 or $50 in side income. But you have to regulate your work to some degree, otherwise you'll end up with nothing but ideas and not a word on paper to show and sell.

Requirements

No special talents beyond a good command of language and imagination are needed to start out, but there's a good deal to learn before you get into the big money. If you have the patience, the self-confidence not to be disillusioned by rejected stories, and the willingness to learn, you can try. They say everybody has at least one good story to tell—and sell!

Future

The number of free-lance writers earning a good living from magazine articles is less than five hundred in the whole country, so this is clearly not a wide-open field. But there are numerous opportunities for the skilled writer to earn $10,000 to $25,000 a year in free-lance work for a variety of employers, either as his or her own boss, or working for a steady salary. And some first-novelists have hit the golden jackpot—the best seller list and sale of movie rights. That's the dream that lures many into this potentially glamorous work.

For Information

On short articles, write Benson Barret Publishers, 6216 North Clark Street, Chicago, Illinois 60626. Or Famous Writers School, Westport, Connecticut 06880, for an aptitude test.

MUSIC AND ENTERTAINMENT

Can you play the piano or guitar, bass fiddle or harmonica? Do you sing or write poems that could be set to music? Many people have these special talents and consider them just a hobby, but they could be put to work to earn extra money for you. If you play an instrument or sing, you can join up with a few other musicians, form your own group, and play for weekend dances, weddings, clubs and parties. If you write lyrics that could become songs, you should try to sell them. You have to love music to go into it in the first place, so this can be one of the most enjoyable jobs in the world. And the greater your skill, the greater the financial rewards— with a little luck.

Earnings

A good, popular local trio, even without an established reputation, can earn $100 to $200 for about three or four hours work, but they have to divide it up, and the total income will hinge on how many nights a week you are engaged.

Hours

Many persons employed full time at other occupations work an occasional night or every weekend to supplement their income in this fun occupation, but the latter part of the week is usually the busiest, and provides the best opportunity for small musical groups. Even church soloists, pianists, and organists find this holds true for wedding jobs.

Requirements

Musical talent is a must, which narrows down the field of candidates for this job, but almost anyone with a good sense of rhythm can learn. You'll also need the instrument, and time to practice.

Future

This is one of those glamorous fields in which the sky is the limit. If you develop the skill, display originality, learn to promote yourself, work hard for years, and have the luck to be discovered, you may become next year's "overnight success" and end up with recording contracts, big-time bookings, and television appearances—all at an unbelievably high pay. On the other hand, if you love music you may be satisfied with any good, steady work in the field.

For Information

Write Taped Instruction International, Post Office Box 735, Times Square Station, New York, New York 10036, for guitar. Or U. S. School of Music, 145 Main Street, Port Washington, New York 11050, for a variety of instruments. For song poems, contact Crown Music Company, 49 West 32nd Street, Studio 340, New York, New York or Songcrafters, 6145 Acklen Station, Nashville, Tennessee.

CARTOONING AND COMMERCIAL ART

Anyone can learn to draw, it's true—just like they say in the ads. But let's face it, you need a little flair, a bit of imagination to make your work profitable. If you keep having ideas for comic strips, political cartoons or jokes, or think you could improve on the advertisements you see in your local newspaper, this could be the job for you. It's exciting, creative work that can be done either in your own home on a spare time basis or in a department store or office.

Earnings

Variations in pay for this work are extreme, from $5 or $10 a week for one local newspaper cartoon to the rich profits of $100 to $200 for syndicating the same cartoon to dozens of newspapers. A talented commercial artist can make $5 to $10 an hour doing part-time work on ads or $100 for a single job. The more creative the work, the higher the pay. Magazines pay $10 to $100 for cartoons.

Hours

Regular or irregular; days, evenings, or weekends.

Requirements

Some talent in art plus a sense of humor.

Future

Top-scale income, self-employed or otherwise.

For Information

Free brochure from Famous American Studios, Spring Park, Minnesota 55384.

FASHION DESIGNING AND MILLINERY

Another pair of creative arts which call for a special flair and an interest in style, with imagination as the vital spark. If you like to experiment, do rough sketches and transform them into real articles of clothing; there are challenging and rewarding fields available to you. You can work at home or sell your abilities to a custom clothing store or manufacturer for a regular income.

Earnings

While milady may balk at a $10 umbrella, there's no budget she won't bend for an original chapeau or one-of-a-kind dress, so depending on your talent and clientele, one sale a week could make this a profitable part-time venture.

Hours

A self-starting occupation that calls for an hour a week or forty-eight, depending on your ambition and desire.

Requirements

If you keep abreast of current trends in fashion and can learn the tricks of the trade, that's all it takes besides talent. A background of sewing, selling clothing, or drawing is helpful.

Future

You can build up your very own hat shop or ladies clothing store, operate from your home on a full-time schedule, or just secure a steady, remunerative career with a large garment firm.

For Information

Write Academy of Millinery Design, Little Falls, New Jersey 07424; or Mayer School of Fashion, 64 West 36th Street, New York, New York 10018.

TEACH DANCING

Are you now or have you ever been a good dancer? Hundreds of people wish someone would teach them, and if you could show them how in the privacy of your home, it could swing a steady part-time income your way. Dancing is fun and teaching it can be, too.

Earnings

For private lessons, people expect to pay $3 to $5 an hour, or you could instruct three to five people at a time for $2 each. Since they would come regularly, once or twice a week, you could count on that much per pupil per week.

Hours

Evening hours usually are the best for this work, since those who want to learn dancing generally have their nights free. But you may be able to arrange classes for housewives in the daytime.

Requirements

If you teach in your home, you'll have to have a sufficiently large and attractive living room, where the rugs can be rolled back, and you'll need a variety of records and a phonograph. Plus the know-how. Or you could work evenings for a local dancing school if there is an opening. Ask!

Future

Dancing changes so much and there are always new young pupils, so a good teacher could build up a steady income from one or two lessons a night, several nights a week. Or it's possible to hire a hall and teach groups of twenty or more, one or two nights a week, for several hours in a row. Add it up, and you'll see why there are so many dancing schools started.

For Information

Contact a local dancing school listed in the Yellow Pages or ask at high schools to see if they'd be interested in having someone teach for a small fee—extra-curricular, of course.

DO ANTIQUES AND FURNITURE REFINISHING

These allied pursuits can be done in a purely speculative way or for a direct, per-job payment; whichever suits you best. If you know an antique from a genuine, worn out piece of furniture, there is plenty of opportunity to make money from your know-how. You can hunt antiques and good, used furniture in second-hand shops and from private sell-outs, refinish them, restore them to their original condition, and then resell for a nice profit. Or you can offer the restoring, refinishing service to furniture owners.

Earnings

For single jobs done for others you could earn up to $5 an hour, less the cost of brushes, stains, and other materials. Or you can really clean up on buying, say, a used $15 dresser and reselling it for $45 after refinishing.

Hours

Set your own; days, evenings, or weekends—a few hours or many.

Requirements

You'll need to know your antiques and how to refinish worn or damaged surfaces, but these skills can be learned easily if you are interested in doing this kind of solitary work, which leaves you pretty much your own boss. You'll need a basement, and a few tools of the trade.

For Information

Many paint stores and unfinished furnitures stores conduct periodic classes in antiquing and refinishing, and you should check locally first. Otherwise write P. Warman, Uniontown, Pennsylvania 15401, about antiques and their prices. Regarding refinishing, write Service Bureau, Popular Mechanics, 575 Lexington Avenue, New York, New York 10022.

BE A BEAUTICIAN, HAIR STYLIST

If you are good at hairdos and have had enough basic training to do the work competently, you could operate your own service, or work for beauty shops, doing a variety of hair arrangements that customers will enjoy and be excited about. There's a wide difference in the amount of talent it takes to put a friend's hair up in curlers and to reshape or recreate a stranger's complete hairdo, but there-in lies a wide range of service and an opportunity to display a flair for beauty if you have it.

Earnings

If you work for yourself, you can charge by the job rather than the hours, and even an at-home shop handling one woman at a time can produce a big income at today's prices. Working by the hour, for somebody else, the pay doesn't reach quite so high, but can be adequate.

Hours

If you work in your home you set the time that an appointment would be convenient for you as well as the customer, but if you work in a shop, hours will be regular, full or part time—morning, afternoons, or evenings, depending on the boss and the traffic.

Requirements

You have to know what you are doing in this work, which is why we call it a special talent. In many cases a regular period of apprenticeship is required by the state and to perform certain tasks in the beauty field there is a registration or licensing. If you are willing to learn and apply yourself as you would to something you are really interested in, the training can be quite brief, considering the rewards.

Future

You can run your own beauty shop at home by procuring basic equipment like driers and small tools, creams, and lotions; or you can offer a home service, charging extra for serving people in their homes. One new specialty that some stay-home beauticians love, because it leaves their hours so flexible, is a wig styling and setting service. People bring their wigs to you, choose a style, and return the next day or at the end of the week for the completed job.

For Information

If you have the talent and background, you are on your way; otherwise, call local beauty shops that look busy and pleasant and ask if they could use a trainee. If you must attend an accredited course in your state, it's best to go through it close to home. Look them up in your telephone book under beauticians or schools. Or see the training section of this book for home study courses in hair styling and beautician work.

BE A TUTOR

Were you ever a school teacher or have you developed on your own a specialty like Civil War lore, a knowledge of politics, government, social studies, or music, or do you know another language? Then you can be a teacher on an individual student basis and earn extra money by sharing your knowledge. High school and college students in public and private institutions often run into trouble in certain classes and can't get all the special attention they need from the teacher, so they must either get special tutoring or flunk.

Earnings

Generally students can't pay too high a rate, but your local schools will be able to supply you with information regarding the range of prices for your service.

Hours

After school hours, late afternoons, evenings, and Saturdays— by appointment, regularly.

Requirements

Obviously, this is a job which requires some special knowledge, and if you don't already have it, unless the learning especially appeals to you, you could apply the time better to another, more profitable pursuit. You also must be able to communicate well, which is the basis for all teaching.

Future

Some college towns support full-time tutoring bureaus, but if this field is a specialty that appeals to you, then full-time teaching work, under contract, is more likely.

For Information

Read and advertise in school papers or any local periodical that circulates among students and their parents. Check if your local textbook stores have a bulletin board you could use to advertise the service. Or telephone the local principal of a school and ask to have teachers refer pupils that need special attention to you.

DO FRAMING

This is really an art, for there is a correct frame for every picture, and it often depends on other furnishings and colors in the room as well as the picture or painting itself. If you have a special touch for this work, or can learn the art's fundamentals quickly by reading about it, and if you like to put things together, you could offer a framing service. Many people have paintings, photos, posters, and mementos around their houses, as well as diplomas, awards, and certificates, and they always say, "I'm going to frame that," but they never get around to doing it themselves.

Earnings

Payment will be by the job and will depend on the size of the picture and the quality of the framing material. You have to allow for your own material costs and time, and adjust your prices accordingly. A dozen routine jobs a week should net you over $20.

Hours

Set your own; you are working for yourself.

Requirements

A little flair for the artistic and good color sense, plus a simple handiness with hammer and cleats. You'll have to invest in at least a sample of various framing materials so the customer can choose, and you'll need little things like wire, brads, cleats, and backing paper.

Future

There are many shops devoted to nothing else but framing, but the most common type of framing store also offers, or at least displays on consignment, a selection of paintings and other articles suitable for framing.

For Information

Check your local adult education class list under art for this specialty, or inquire at a framing material or hobby store where they would show you the basics in exchange for your business in buying materials there.

TRY INVENTING AND THINKING

Yes, thinking. Ideas are worth money. If inventing things is your hobby or thinking about better ways to do things is a natural inclination for you, why not put yourself to work for you as an idea man. Many firms are constantly searching the country looking for new ideas that can be put onto the market at a profit to themselves, as well as the inventor. And, as they say, all it takes is a better mousetrap. As for ideas and their application, often you have to seek out the firm which could best benefit from the idea.

Earnings

From zero to millions, depending on what you come up with and its market value.

Hours

Completely your own.

Requirements

An imaginative, active mind which has the curiosity to examine things and systems and ask the question, "Why don't they do it differently?"

Future

Millionaires and poor dreamers both belong to this occupational class, so the potential is enormous.

For Information

Write American Amateur Inventors Club, William J. Lawson, Poteet, Texas 78065; or Raymond Lee, Invention Developer, 230-P Park Avenue, New York, New York 10017.

TRY CATERING AND COOKING

If you can bake a cake, whip up a superb meal, or just manage the directions on a cake-mix box, with the help of a good oven, you may be able to bring in plenty of extra income by cooking and baking for others. Sometimes small parties for children or adults can be catered so that the parents are free to play with the children, or so that nobody is tied up in the kitchen. There are many calls for cakes—birthdays, anniversaries, weddings, etc—with the simple, special wording in icing personalizing them. Restaurants are big business, so even the average home oven can produce a good income if it's run right. Think about the kind of cooking that might be most in demand in your community and in the circle of your acquaintance, and specialize; that's the best advice for beginners in this potentially profitable field.

Earnings

Your income will vary widely, depending on whether you bake one cake for $2 after spending $.50 on ingredients, or if you bake ten cakes in a day at the same rate. If you serve a whole birthday party for twenty kiddies, with cake, cookies, punch, and ice cream, with a little favor of candy and a few streamers tossed in, you could ask a dollar per child and most people would consider it fair. Deducting ingredients and expenses, your profit would be about $15, and your work would not have been much more than a couple hours, not counting oven time, during which you can be doing anything you please.

Hours

You'll have to arrange your hours so that the party food or cake involved arrives on time and fresh, but otherwise your time can be apportioned according to your own whim.

Requirements

If you can cook just a few specialties, you can handle this part-time work, with only one rule: don't experiment on new dishes with customers. An oven, a few basic ingredients, and the initiative to let the right people know your talent is available for hire from time to time.

Future

If business gets better and better, you may be headed toward full-time restaurant operation or catering service.

For Information

To start this part-time work, the first step is to examine the marketing possibilities in your community or neighborhood. A couple of examples: one woman who lives in a college town makes an excellent supplemental income by securing birthdates and parents' addresses of students, through the approved channels at the colleges; then she sends notes to the parents and offers to bake a personalized cake for their son or daughter and deliver it on his or her birthday for the price of $3.50. She gets an amazing 55 per cent of orders on her queries, and with so many orders, she bakes an average of a cake a day, for about $25 a week spare time income, less ingredients. Another woman who lives near a local children's park and has a large, suitable room, hosts parties for groups of children in her home. The children convene for their cake and other goodies, then dash across to the park with their gift balloons and wind up the event with a play session using the park's facilities. Many people don't want to bake, especially in the hot summer months, so just a service that advertises "Cakes for All Occasions—Including Dessert," might be profitable in your neighborhood.

BE A TYPIST

Proficiency with a typewriter can and does earn many a full-time living, and it can do the same on a part-time basis, too, either working for hard-pressed local companies or doing typing jobs at home for special customers who are contacted by advertising. Unless you commit yourself to a big rush job, you can work whatever spare hours are convenient.

Earnings

Working for somebody else, a typist may earn about $2.60 an hour or more, by the hour, on a part-time basis. Working at home on jobs she or he solicits by himself, the pay can be much better. Simple manuscript typing, with one carbon copy, can earn $.35 a page with a competent ten pages an hour, at least. Some typists charge $.50 and up to $.75 a page for more complicated typing which slows down the pace.

Hours

Set your own deadline and hours for finishing each job.

Requirements

Typewriter and ability to use it plus reliability.

Future

Full-time work.

For Information

List your service with local schools and colleges, as well as any writers' clubs. Don't overlook such work as regular monthly billing for doctors or companies in your town. Or write for booklet, typing for profit, Quest Enterprises, Post Office Box 6029, San Jose, California 95150.

Chapter 7
ANYONE CAN LEARN

The best-paying, most secure jobs on earth are those that require a special skill or know-how; once you've got it, your income, prestige, and whole way of life move up because you are in
a select category. There may be 200,000,000 people in America,
but there are only about 870,000 contractors and 3,000,000 building trades workers. When you hear that 42 per cent more drafts-
men will be needed in the next ten years, or that the burgeoning
travel field is expanding 15 per cent every year, or that thousands
of job openings are going begging in the computer industry and
electronics, you know that the people involved in these specialties
will be making more and more money and be more and more in
demand.

While your need for moonlighting may be a temporary one, this
may be the time to take a good, hard look at your future and your
resources for controlling it. The cost of living keeps going up, which
makes moonlighting necessary for so many millions of people, but
those who master a special trade or profession are the men and
women who will keep abreast of the times and really get ahead
economically. So whether you are interested in spare time pursuits
now, or full-time profits for the rest of your life, carefully consider the advantages of learning some specialty that will assure
you never are caught without a sure-fire way to a comfortable
income, via pleasurable work.

Most of the jobs which you can learn at home in your spare
time have a number of common advantages:

High Earnings
Once you have acquired the necessary know-how, you can count
on a definite per-hour income, guaranteed by the fact that you
have a skill which industries and businesses are crying for. Most
of the jobs, full-time, are in the $10,000-a-year-and-up bracket.

Hours

Having a specialty that is much in demand permits you to bargain for the hours you want, thus most of these jobs can be pursued either full time for companies or part time, working with your home as your office.

Requirements

If you have the ability to study and learn, you don't even need a high school education to qualify for many of these high-paying jobs, and special aptitude tests are offered free in most cases where a decided inclination is indicated. You'll need a few hours to study at home, a small investment in the course for your future, and one very necessary element—interest in the type of work you will be doing. Pick something you think you would like, some job you would enjoy doing.

Future

In most cases, income security is the outstanding appeal of these jobs, but apart from the attraction of steady part-time or full-time work, they all offer the distinct advantage of lending themselves easily to the chance of going into business for yourself, as described in Chapter 8.

We will list a few of the representative jobs you may enter via home study, but remember, there are many more, and a thorough perusal of the school listings will give you an idea of just how many there are. Although some of the fields in which job training are offered may be listed elsewhere is this book, the determining factor in most cases is this: that without training in the field, chances of finding work in the specific occupation would be negligible. Many tasks are learned by apprenticeship or on-the-job training, but in these cases, home study is probably the quickest, least expensive route:

BROADCASTER

A clear voice and distinct pronunciation are all that you need to learn the tricks of the trade and break into the fast-growing fields of radio and television communication. There are high-paying part and full-time jobs open everywhere in commercials, sportscasting, news delivery, announcing, and disc jockeying. In major cities some of these positions require union membership.

TECHNICAL WRITER

Thousands of people are needed to fill positions translating the complicated language of the medical, science, electronics, and aerospace industries into readable English for pamphlets, textbooks, and manuals. One of the most secure of all writing jobs.

TELEVISION, HI-FI, RADIO REPAIRMAN

Repairs and installations have brought part-time and full-time profits to dozens of people in practically every community in the country, and now that nearly every home has more than one television set, radio, or phonograph, there are millions of specialists required in the field.

WELDER

Not difficult to learn, and adaptable to many industries—automotive, aerospace, marine, manufacture, and repair. The tools do the work when you learn to handle them.

AUTOMOBILE MECHANIC

You might learn this at a service station or garage in your local area, but if you are to become a top-level mechanic and get all that goes with it, sooner or later you'll have to master the manuals and books that show the proven, easy ways to locate the trouble and correct it. If you like cars, you'll love this job.

BOOKKEEPER

In a world buried in paperwork most of it too complicated for nonspecialists, there are thousands upon thousands of opportunities for those who like working with figures. Tax computations, general accounting, inventory control, and regular business record keeping afford a steady job or a part-time occupation for anyone who knows how.

STENOTYPIST

An allied profession that puts you in line for high pay as the operator of a basic business machine that records court proceedings, official hearings, and similar sessions. Operation of other business equipment, such as comptometers, cash registers, and teletypes also can be profitable.

CLAIMS ADJUSTER

Seldom a part-time job, but one that offers considerable latitude in when and where you work, this specialty has grown as fast as the automobile business. Investigators of traffic accidents and other insurance claims are highly valued by their employers.

AIR CONDITIONING AND HEATING

Learning both of these related jobs keeps you working summer and winter on installations and repairs, either as your own boss, or for a good wage with a company in the business.

DRAFTSMAN

Experts in architectural or mechanical drafting, drawing the blueprints which builders and manufacturers turn into reality, ride a high-paid wave of surging mass production and home construction, which leads to bigger and better jobs for them from one year to the next. Everything they learn adds to their income.

MEDICAL ASSISTANT

A highly scientific occupation which requires thousands of trained secretaries and technicians for medical doctors, dentists, and hospitals. Once you learn the language and equipment used by doctors and medical specialists, you're on your way to good, steady pay working for them in a variety of tasks, part time or full time.

COMPUTER PROGRAMMER

No field today is more inviting than this one. The computer invasion reaches into every phase of life, from the universities and big businesses to the corner bank and even our love life via computer dating. Those who can learn machine operation, data processing, and wiring are putting themselves in line for continuing promotions in bigger and better jobs.

ELECTRICIAN, ELECTRONICS OR RADAR EXPERT

Unless you acquire these trades through military service or long apprenticeships, there's no other way then a course of study, but almost anyone can learn at home. From the home wiring electrician to the expert in complex radar systems, all can count on a secure, permanent job with all signals "Go."

CARPENTER, MASON, PLUMBER

These other building construction trades can be seasonal in some parts of the country, or many be heavily controlled by unions. But those who master the arts are always in demand in the booming home, store, and office building contruction and remodeling fields, with a steady $5 an hour or more as their base pay. You work with tools, alone or with others, on your own or for others.

ENGINEER

One of the longest listings in the want ad sections of newspapers throughout this country is for engineers. They are so much in demand that employers fight for them, woo them, and win them with high pay and numberous other benefits. Structural engineers, civil engineers, mechanical engineers, design engineers, marine engineers, electrical engineers—and the variety and appeal of the work is endless.

ENGRAVER

A little art helps in this techical specialty and a good engraver is always in demand, so much as that he can decide if he'll work on his own, part time, or full time for somebody else. Good steady work and job satisfaction.

DRY CLEANER

If you want to open your own shop, and even the smaller communities have more than one because there is so much business, you can learn the ins and outs of this profitable occupation by mail.

For information of these specialties and many, many more, contact the appropriate school or firm listed below. Most are approved and accredited by the National Home Study Council and/or their state or local departments of public instruction:

Academy of Millinery Design, Little Falls, New Jersey 07424. Professional custom millinery. A division of Technical Home Study Schools.

Advance Trades School, 5944 North Newark Avenue, Chicago, Illinois 60631. Electricity, electrical service, and appliance repair, motor winding wiring; mobile engine service; automobile, truck, tractor; diesel and small gasoline engine repair; refrigeration and air conditioning service; electricity, servicing motors and installation; service and maintenance of industrial, commercial, residential, automotive air conditioning and refrigeration, including air conditioners, food freezers and dehumidifiers; bookkeeping; elementary accounting.

Airline Personnel Training by Humboldt, Inc., 2201 Blaisdell Avenue, South, Minneapolis, Minnesota 55404. Preparation for airline resident training covers courses for station agent, communications, passenger agent reservations, air freight agent, operations, ticket agents, tour and travel. An affiliate of Humboldt Institute.

Allied Institute of Technology, 1338-42 South Michigan Avenue, Chicago, Illinois 60605. Air conditioning, heating, and refrigeration; auto mechanics and service; machine shop practice and blueprint reading; mechanical drafting and elements of design; engineering drafting technology; industrial tool engineering, tool and die design.

American Association of Medical Record Librarians, 211 East Chicago Avenue, Chicago, Illinois 60611. Correspondence course for medical record personnel, an in-service training program in twenty-five lessons for persons engaged in medical record work in hospitals and clinics.

American Automation Training Centers, 2022 Main Street, Kansas City, Missouri 64108. Computer operation and programming taught for jobs in aerospace, medicine, industries, and retailing.

American Landscape School, 4040 42nd Street, Des Moines, Iowa 50310. Landscaping and gardening for professionals and non-professionals; nursery work, gardening design, and industrial landscape plans.

American School, Drexel Avenue at 58th Street, Chicago, Illinois 60637. Thirty-two basic courses containing three hundred subjects: agriculture; apprentice training; architecture; contracting; building; plumbing; automobile mechanics; business management; retail merchandising; corporation finance; auditing; accounting salesmanship; bookkeeping; secretarial; diesel mechanics; drafting; electrician; electrical technician; instrumentation; computers; transistors; industrial sound systems; electronic communication (includes FCC License preparation); magnetic amplifiers; industrial electronics; civil, electrical, mechanical engineering; surveying; foremanship; human relations; metal working; machinist; blueprint reading; tool design; pattern and foundry; sheet metal; ammonia refrigeration; rigging; industrial hydraulics.

American School of Photography, 835 Diversey Parkway, Chicago, Illinois 60614. Portrait, commercial, and color photography; motion picture, and news photography.

American Technical Society, 850 East 58th Street, Chicago, Illinois 60637. Vocational training in accounting, tool design, drafting, auto mechanics, bookkeeping, building, contracting, business administration, carpentry, drafting, electricity, electronics, foremanship, machine shop work, merchandising, secretarial, selling, and welding.

American Tuning School, Gilroy, California 95020. Home study in piano tuning.

Anderson School of Scientific Massage, Princeton, Illinois. Professional massage taught by mail; diploma awarded.

Art Instruction Schools, 500 South Fourth Street, Minneapolis, Minnesota 55415. Specialized courses in four separate commercial art fields: advertising art; illustrating; cartooning; and painting. Each course includes complete coverage of basic art subjects, areas of specialization in a major art field, and a variety of elective subjects selected to meet the needs of each individual student.

Atlantic Educational Aids, Box 6086, North Augusta, South Carolina 29841. Typing; a ten-lesson recorded course.

Atlantic School, 2020 Grand Avenue, Kansas City, Missouri 64108. Airline career training: a combination home study-resident course for men and women in airline operations, reservations, ticketing, communications, passenger service, hostess, tariff, automation, air cargo, clerical, and other tour, travel and transportation services.

Automation Training, Inc., 6600 Delmar, St. Louis, Missouri 63130. Courses offered in tabulation and wiring and a combination course of tabulation and wiring and computer programming. Lessons are based on IBM equipment.

Belsaw Institute, 315 Westport Road, Kansas City, Missouri 64111. Locksmithing; vocational training with tools and supplies; starting and developing own business as skilled locksmith.

Blackstone School of Law, 307 North Mighigan Avenue, Chicago, Illinois 60601. Home study leading to professional Bachelor of Laws degree.

Boston Institute, 1108 Beacon Street, Newton, Massachusetts. Fundamentals of medical secretary career.

Britannica Schools, Inc., 425 North Michigan Avenue, Chicago, Illinois 60611. Subjects include writing, technical writing, and bookkeeping. Britannica Institute for Executive Development: management training including effective executive practices; understanding computers; data processing systems; advanced office machines; scientific techniques for evaluation and decision making; corporation finance; banking; insurance; investment practices; accounting processes; business law; and marketing. A subsidiary of Encyclopaedia Britannica, Inc.

Business Electronics, 209 West Jackson Boulevard, Chicago, Illinois 60606. Programming for digital computers; includes programming technology and systems design in terms of business applications.

Canadian Institute of Science and Technology, 263 Adelaide Street West, Toronto, Canada.

The Capitol Radio Engineering Institute (CREI), 3224 Sixteenth Street, North West Washington, D.C. 20010. Complete diploma programs including electronic engineering technology and special programs for engineers with specialized study of major electives such as communications; aeronautical and navigational engineering; television; servomechanisms; radar; and various space technology. Other diploma programs in nuclear engineering technology; computer systems technology; and industrial electronics for engineers. Certificate programs in advanced mathematics and principles of leadership.

Capitol Tuning School, 3160 S.W. 16th Court, Ft. Lauderdale, Fla. Home course in piano tuning.

Career Academy, 825 North Jefferson Street, Milwaukee, Wisconsin 53202. Offers courses in medical office assisting and radio and television broadcasting.

Career Academy's Division of Investment Banking, 825 North Jefferson Street, Milwaukee, Wisconsin 53202. Home studies in nonselling operations in field of stocks, bonds, and investments.

Central Technical Institute, 1644 Wyandotte Street, Kansas City, Missouri 64108. Electronic technology; radio operator course; television servicing course; computer programming; airline agent training; airline transportation career training; business automation training; electronic engineering technology.

Chicago School of Interior Decoration, 835 Diversey Parkway, Chicago, Illinois 60614. Interior decoration for the professional decorator, related sales personnel, or for personal use.

Chicago School of Watchmaking, Fox River Grove, Illinois 60021. Home study system for learning watch and lcock repairing at home.

Chicago Technical College, 2000 South Michigan Avenue, Chicago, Illinois 60616. Machine, architectural, electrical, and structural drafting and design; building construction; blueprint reading; estimating; and foremanship.

Cleveland Institute of Electronics, 1776 East 17th Street, Cleveland, Ohio 33113. Electronics technology; industrial electronics and automation; broadcast engineering; first class FCC license; electronic communications (including 2nd class FCC License); carrier telephony; electronic slide rule and operation; math for electronics; advanced communication engineering.

Commercial Trades Institute, 1400 West Greenleaf Avenue, Chicago, Illinois 60626. Refrigeration, air conditioning and heating; service, installation, and maintenance; automotive air conditioning; successful business practices; tools and equipment furnished for practical experience. Automotive mechanics overhaul and tune-up; automatic transmissions; diesel or body and fender repair option; thirty job experience projects, including tools and testing equipment. Television electronics; service and repair; color TV; transistors and printed circuits; kits for building testing instruments, TV receiver included; industrial electronics, service and maintenance kits for building testing instruments included; building construction, covering all phases of the building trades for the contractor, including estimating, financing, plumbing, heating, wiring, carpentry, masonry and landscaping.

De Vry Technical Institute, 4141 Belmont Avenue, Chicago, Illinois 60641. Electronic space and missile instruments; computer control electronics; electronic control systems; electronic instrumentation; electronic communications, including radar, FCC License preparation, and broadcasting; integrated circuitry; television-radio servicing, including color television; electronic automation technology; automotive electricity.

Doll Hospital School, 2251 Barry Avenue, Los Angeles, California 90064. Courses in doll repairs, doll making, clothing, shop operations.

Educational Institute of the American Hotel and Motel Association, Michigan State University, Kellogg Center, East Lansing, Michigan 48823. Hotel and motel management; front office procedure; accounting; economy; law sales promotion; communications; motor hotel and motel management human relations; housekeeping, maintenance and engineering. Food and beverage management; purchasing controls; management; and service.

Engraving Division, Warner Electric, 1512 Jarvis Avenue, Chicago, Illinois 60626. Home-taught engraving system.

Famous American Studios, Spring Park, Minnesota 55384. Learn cartooning and commercial art.

Famous Artists Schools, Westport, Connecticut 06880. Professional art courses: commercial art; illustration and design; fine arts paintings; editorial and commercial cartooning. Comprehensive art course for talented young people.

Famous Photographers School, Westport, Connecticut 06881. Creative and advanced techniques of modern photography; theory, principles, and professional skills, and practices.

Famous Writers School, Westport, Connecticut 06881. Fiction; nonfiction; advertising; and business writing. The first three courses include writing for television.

Gemological Institute of America, 11940 San Vicente Boulevard, Los Angeles, California 90049. Courses on identifying, grading, and appraising diamonds and colored stones; jewelry designing and jewelry retailing.

Good Dressmaking Institute, 2251 Barry Avenue, Los Angeles, California 90064. Courses in modern dressmaking.

Grantham School of Electronics, 1505 North Western Avenue, Hollywood, California 90027. Basic electricity; basic electronics; communications electronics; microwave electronics; and electronics engineering technology.

Hemphill Schools, 1584 West Washington Boulevard, Los Angeles, California 90007. (All courses offered in Spanish language.) Programs for training technicians and service personnel in radio-television-electronics; automotive mechanics; diesel engine mechanics; electrical and commercial appliances; basic and advanced conversational English with audio aids.

Hill's Business University, 629 West Main Street, Oklahoma City, Oklahoma 73102. Bookkeeping; all branches of accounting; secretarial; stenographic and allied subjects; shorthand, Gregg or machine; court and convention reporting; computer programming and data processing.

The Holmes Institute, 3224 Sixteenth Street, North West, Washington, D.C. 20010. Principles of leadership program designed for technical personnel planning to take on supervisory and management responsibilities.

Industrial Training Institute, Inc., 815 East Rosecrans Avenue, Los Angeles, California 90059. Programs for training technicians and service personnel in the following electrical, electronic, radio-television subjects; basic electronics; industrial electronics, including automation and computers; radio-television electronics service, including FM, transistors and color television; basic electricity; domestic, commercial and industrial electricity; electrical appliance servicing.

Industrial Training School, Inc., 11130 Grand River Avenue, Detroit, Michigan 48204. Courses in time-study methods, engineering, and industrial supervision.

Institute of Applied Science, 1920 Sunnyside Avenue, Chicago, Illinois 60640. Criminal and civil identification and investigation in law enforcement agencies, private detective agencies, and plant protection; course includes fingerprinting, police photography, investigation, identification of handwriting, typewriting, and firearms.

International Accountants Society, Inc., 209 West Jackson Boulevard, Chicago, Illinois 60606. All branches of accounting: elementary, intermediate and advanced, including auditing; corporation finance; CPA coaching; income tax; cost accounting; office management; economics; management control.

International Correspondence Schools, Scranton, Pennsylvania 18515. Over 225 courses: accounting, including CPA training; advertising; air conditioning; apprentice training; architecture; art; automobile; business administration; building trades; college level courses; chemical, civil, electrical, industrial, mechanical, and stationary engineering; commercial; communication technology; computer programming and COBOL; data processing and systems; diesel engines; drafting and blueprint reading; electrician; electric motor repair; electronic computers; electronics; FCC license preparation; FORTRAN; foundry; heating; high school; industrial telemetering; instrumentation; interior decoration; inventory control; machine and tool design; mapping; mathematics (through calculus); pattern-making; physics; petroleum; plumbing; pulp and paper; radio and television; refrigeration; retailing; salesmanship; secretarial; sheet metal; shop practice; short story writing; statistics; supervision; surveying; telephony; textile; traffic management; welding.

Interstate Training Service, 4035 North East Sandy Boulevard, Portland, Oregon 97212. Basic diesel apprentice and mechanic course in operation, maintenance, repair and rebuild of diesel engines, with terminal training at Cummins Engine Company factory; specialized component and product education training on trucks, caterpillar tractors, I.H. tractors, heavy equipment, diesel engines, and fuel injection equipment. General course in diesel, tractor, and heavy equipment operation, maintenance, and repair. Handcraft courses in plastics, metalcraft, and woodworking (cabinet making).

LaSalle Extension University, 417 South Dearborn Street, Chicago, Illinois 60605. (Divisions: Utilities Engineering Institute and Wayne School). Accounting training: introductory, intermediate, and advanced general professional accounting; auditing, cost, controllership, systems, tax accounting; and CPA training. American law and procedure training for leadership; including business law, contract law, insurance law, law for claim representatives, law for police officers, law for trust officers, and real estate law. Business management training; advertising and sales promotion; basic, finacial, office personnel, production, and sales management; computer programming. Dental assistant training; dental assisting techniques and office management. Drafting; basic, aeronautical, architectural, electrical, mechanical, and structural drafting. High school; general diploma courses including specialized vocational fields. Interior decorating; design and decoration, business practices, and procedures. Real estate training; real estate brokerage, investment, management, planning, sales. Sales training; secretarial training; office procedures; typing; shorthand; stenotype (machine shorthand) training. Technical vocational training: air conditioning, refrigeration, and heating; diesel; mechanical refrigeration. Traffic and transportation training: organization and management; freight classification; rates and tariffs; transportation agencies and services; transportation law and regulations; rate making; and rate cases.

Lewis Hotel-Motel Training School, 2301 Pennsylvania Avenue, North West Washington, D.C. 20037. Fifty-two lessons covering hotel, motel, club, restaurant, institution, and apartment management. Subjects include front office; communications; housekeeping; menu planning; purchasing; food and beverage control; dining room service and management; maintenance and sanitation; advertising and public relations; sales management; practical psychology; social programming; and accounting procedures.

Lifetime Career Schools, 2251 Barry Avenue, Los Angeles, California 90064. Five courses: National Landscape Institute; residential and commercial landscaping. National Floral Institute; flower arranging and floral shop operations. Good Dressmaking Institute;

modern dressmaking. Doll Hospital School; doll repairs, doll making, clothing, shop operations. Decorative arts and crafts course.

Lincoln Extension Institute, 1401 West 75th Street, Cleveland, Ohio 44102. More than twenty management courses for business and industry. Preparing for promotion; developing personality; developing management leadership; manager's job; management-labor relations; personnel management; practical sketching for managers; practical math; industrial materials handling; materials handling and plant layout; time study and methods improvement; work simplification; job evaluation; merit rating; production planning and control; product engineering and control; quality and reliability control; accounting—tool for managerial control; accounting fundamentals for the nonaccountant; introduction to data processing; understanding use of computers; managing a data processing department; management organization and control; profit planning for management.

Lincoln-Technical Institute, 427 Market Street, Newark, New Jersey. Small engine repair for outboards, powermowers, chain saws, and similar jobs.

Locksmithing Institute, Little Falls, New Jersey 07424. Locksmithing and key making. A division of Technical Home Study Schools.

Massey Technical Institute, 148 East 7th Street, Jacksonville, Florida 32206. Radio, television, and industrial electronic equipment servicing; communications; bookkeeping and accounting.

Mayer School of Fashion, 64 West 36th Street, New York, New York 10018. Home study in fashion designing, dressmaking, draping, sketching, and patternmaking.

Metals Engineering Institute, American Society for Metals, Metals Park, Ohio 44073. Twenty-three courses dealing with the metallurgical aspects of heat treatment, welding, foundry, electroplating corrosion, steelmaking, nonferrous metals, high temperature alloys, nuclear materials, machining, and others.

National Baking School, 835 Diversey Parkway, Chicago, Illinois 60614. Modern baking practices and management.

National Camera Repair School, 2000 West Union Street, Englewood, Colorado 80110. Camera repair; technical and avocational, with tools and practice equipment. Terminal resident training available.

National Career Center, 3839 White Plains Road, Bronx, New York, 10467. For facts on jobs in business, beauty culture, or men's hair styling and recommended schools near your home. Ten cents for brochure.

National Floral Institute, 2251 Barry Avenue, Los Angeles, California 90064. Courses in flower arranging and floral shop operations.

National Institute of Drycleaning, Correspondence School, 909 Burlington Avenue, Silver Spring, Maryland 20910. Five courses cover fiber and fabric properties; stain removal procedures; petroleum and synthetic drycleaning methods; sales training for counter or route sales people.

National Landscape Institute, 2251 Barry Avenue, Los Angeles, California 90064. Courses in residential and commercial landscaping.

National Photo Coloring School, 835 Diversey Parkway, Chicago, Illinois 60614. Coloring photographs and miniatures in oil.

National Photo/Phonics School, 2000 West Union Street, Englewood, Colorado 80110. Teaches the skills necessary to plan and produce audio-visual presentations. Includes budgeting; script writing; photography (both still and motion picture); sound effects; and recording.

National Radio Institute, 3939 Wisconsin Avenue, North West, Washington, D.C. 20016. Eleven courses in electronics; radio-television servicing; advanced color TV servicing; complete communications; industrial-military electronics; FCC license; basic electronics; applied mathematics in electronics; electronics for automation; aircraft communications and guidance; marine communications; mobile communications. Electrical appliance servicing, including small gasoline engine repair, air conditioning and refrigeration.

Safety Training Institute, National Safety Council, 425 North Michigan Avenue, Chicago, Illinois 60611. Supervising for safety; a basic accident prevention course for foremen. Includes human relations, materials handling and storage, job instruction, and fire prevention.

National School of Dress Design, 835 Diversey Parkway, Chicago, Illinois 60614. Course includes costume design, fashion sketching, pattern drafting, cutting, and fitting.

National School of Forestry and Conservation, 2000 P. Street, North West, Washington, D.C. 20036. Three courses in forestry, fish, wildlife, and park conservation; soil, water, and range conservation; to prepare men and women for vocational jobs to improve laymen's understanding of natural processes, and to aid landowners in the management of their land.

National School of Home Study, 229 Park Avenue South, New York, New York 10003. Special vocational courses: bookkeeping; typewriting and shorthand; private secretary; mathematics; home management; dressmaking and design; filing and others.

National Tax Training School, Monsey, New York 10952. Federal income tax course; covers individual and small business tax law; procedures; tax savings; return preparation; payroll taxes; establishment and operation of tax practice. Higher course in federal taxes: covers partnership; corporation, estate, and excise taxes. Social Security course: includes coverage requirements; obtaining maximum benefits; retirement planning; procedure before the Social Security Administration.

National Technical Schools, 4000 South Figueroa Street, Los Angeles, California 90037. Courses in: electronics-TV-Radio servicing and communications; master course in electronics-TV-radio, plus advanced TV and industrial electronics; master course in color television; color television servicing; FCC license course; radio servicing AM-FM-transistor; television servicing (including color lessons); stereo, hi-fi, and sound systems; basic electronics; electronics math. Automotive-diesel master course; automotive mechanics; diesel mechanics; engine tune-up and automotive electricity—courses include repair and overhaul of gasoline, diesel and gas turbine engines; carburetion; auto electricity; engine tune-up; automatic transmission; power assemblies; diesel fuel injection; all automotive chassis units. Air conditioning, refrigeration, and electrical appliances—course includes servicing home refrigeration; room and centralized air conditioning; automobile air conditioners; all popular portable and major electrical appliances. Home appliance technician's course—includes heating appliances of all kinds; motor-operated appliances; home refrigerators; washing machines; clothes dryers, and other major appliances.

Nelson-Hall Company, 325 West Jackson Boulevard, Chicago, Illinois 60606. Locksmithing and key making.

New York Institute of Photography, 10 West 33rd Street, New York, New York 10001. All phases of modern photography, including: commercial; news; creative pictorialism; fashion; architectural; landscape; portrait; figure study; child portraiture; bridal; photo oil coloring; retouching; darkroom techniques; all currently employed natural color processes; motion picture; careers in photography; studio business methods.

New York School of Interior Design, 155 East 56th Street, New York, New York 10022. Home study course in interior design and residential decorating.

New York School of Writing, 630 Ninth Avenue, New York, New York 10036. Home study courses leading to well-paying jobs in writing.

Newspaper Institute of America, 2 Park Avenue, New York, New York 10016. Journalism; feature article and fiction writing; poetry; short story writing; writing for radio, TV, and films; dramatic writing; and specialized writing including advertising, religious, social business, club scientific, and industrial.

North American Institute of Systems and Procedures, 4401 Birch Street, Newport, California 92660. Courses on charting; procedure planning; forms design; office layout; computer programming; and data processing systems.

Niles Bryant School, 3631 Stockton Boulevard, Sacramento, California 95820. Piano tuning; piano action regulating; and piano repair.

North American School of Advertising, University Plaza, Campus Drive, Newport Beach, California 92660. A complete fifty-seven lesson course in advertising and public relations offered to prepare students for careers in advertising departments, advertising agencies, media, and allied advertising fields. The course includes training in copyrighting; commercial art; production; media; research; campaigns; administration and organization; mail order; and public relations.

North American School of Conservation, University Plaza, Campus Drive, Newport Beach, California 92660. Courses offered prepare men for vocational careers with federal, state, and private organizations. One hundred lesson course covers all phases of conservation including instruction in wildlife management; fish management; forest management; park management; and soil and range management.

North American School of Drafting, 4500 Campus Drive, University Plaza, Newport Beach, California 92660. Architectural and mechanical draftsmanship.

North American School of Flocking and Screen Process Printing, 4401 Birch Street, Newport Beach, California 92660. Course offered to prepare students for careers in printing, refinishing, and decorating. A thirty-eight lesson vocational trade course in the arts of flocking and silk screen process printing.

North American School of Travel, 4500 Campus Drive, Newport Beach, California 92660. Opportunities in the travel field: including agencies; tour planning; air, sea, and land tours.

Palmer Writers School, 500 South Fourth Street, Minneapolis, Minnesota 55415. Specialized courses in fiction writing; nonfiction writing; article writing; radio writing; and television writing. Each course includes complete coverage of basic writing subjects, areas of specialization, and a variety of elective subjects selected to meet the needs of each individual student.

Philco Technical Institute, 219 North Broad Street, Philadelphia, Pennsylvania 19107. Offers advanced programs for the experienced technician and field engineer. Courses are solid-state electronics; digital computer fundamentals; and programming for digital computers.

RCA Institutes, 320 West 31st Street, New York, New York 10001. Home study programs in television servicing; telecommunications; FCC license preparation; electronics drafting; automation electronics; automatic controls; digital techniques; industrial electronics; nuclear instrumentation; and solid state electronics.

Radio Television Training of America, 229 Park Avenue South, New York, New York 10003. Electronics technician; control room technician; radio, FM, and TV technician; color TV technician; advanced techniques of TV servicing; transistors and printed circuits; business practices for the TV service dealer; FCC coaching course; TV studio technician course; advanced techniques of radio servicing.

Sales Training of Southern California, 1650 Wilshire Boulevard, Los Angeles 90017. Proven sales techniques in mail courses.

School of Famous Broadcasters, 825 North Jefferson Street, Milwaukee, Wisconsin 53202. Courses in radio and television broadcasting.

School of Modern Photography, Little Falls, New Jersey 07424. Photography course including: principles; darkroom techniques; commercial; portrait; news; movie; and color.

School of Speedwriting, 55 West 42nd Street, New York, New York 10036. Learn speedwriting shorthand at home in your spare time.

The Slip Cover School, Little Falls, New Jersey 07424. Making custom furniture clip covers.

Taped Instruction-International, Post Office Box 735, Times Square Station, New York, New York 10036. Guitar lessons; folk, pop, and rock.

Technical Home Study School, Little Falls, New Jersey 07424. Academy of Millinery Design: professional custom millinery. Locksmithing Institute: locksmithing and key making. School of Modern Photography: photography principles and darkroom techniques; commercial portrait; news; movie; and color. The Slip Cover School: making custom furniture slip covers. Typewriter Repair School: typewriter repair. Upholstery Trades School: custom furniture upholstery.

Technical Training International, Inc., 10447 South Torrence Avenue, Chicago, Illinois 60617. Electronics: electronics training covering introductory, basic, advanced, radio and TV, and industrial. Diesel: service; repair; overhaul; maintenance and operation of internal combustion engines; diesel, industrial, and agricultural tractors and heavy equipment.

Typewriter Repair School, Little Falls, New Jersey 07424. Typewriter repair.

Upholstery Trades School, Little Falls, New Jersey 07424. Custom furniture upholstery, includes practice materials.

U.S. School of Music, 145 Main Street, Port Washington, New York 11050. Piano; guitar; accordion; violin; organ (pipe and electronic); steel guitar; mandolin; ukulele; saxophone, tenor banjo; trumpet; cornet; trombone; clarinet; elementary harmony; isometric finger control.

Universal Airlines Personnel Schools, 1872 Northwest 7th Street, Miami, Florida 33125. Training at home in communications; passenger service; reservations; ticketing; operations; and hostess.

Universal Motel Schools, 1872 Northwest 7th Street, Miami, Florida 33125. Courses in motel management and operation.

Utilities Engineering Institute, 417 South Dearborn Street, Chicago, Illinois 60605. Technical vocational training in air conditioning, refrigeration, heating diesel.

Van Brook Company, Oregon, Illinois 61061. New pictorial method shows step-by-step piano tuning by mail.

Washington School of Art, 145 Main Street, Port Washington, New York 11050. General art course in drawing; painting; illustration; advertising art; cartooning; fashion; TV art.

Wayne School, 417 South Dearborn Street, Chicago, Illinois 60605. Dental assisting and general diploma high school courses, including specialized vocational fields.

Weaver Airline Personnel School, 3521 Broadway, Kansas City, Missouri 64111. Airline personnel training exclusively: hostess; reservations; communication; station agent; passenger agent; and radio operator positions.

Weaver School of Real Estate, 3521 Broadway, Kansas City, Missouri 64111. Real estate buying; selling; appraisal; management; in preparation for salesmen's and brokers' licenses.

Women's Institute for Continuing Study, Scranton, Pennsylvania 18515. Accounting; advertising; art and design; chemistry; commerical; computer programming and COBOL; drafting; English; high school; interior decorating; languages; management; salesmanship; secretarial; supervision; personality development.

Writer's Digest, 22 East 12th Street, Cincinnati, Ohio 45210. Courses in short story writing; short-short story writing; article writing.

Chapter 8

THE FUTURE—WHY NOT GO INTO BUSINESS FOR YOURSELF?

If you can find financial success through moonlighting, and surely one of the scores of attractive jobs described in this book will show you the way, then you might consider this: Why not make your moonlighting job your future career?

In the first place, the wise moonlighter has chosen a part-time endeavor which appeals to him, perhaps more than his full-time pursuit, and if this is the situation in your case, there is no reason why you could not build a whole new life, and a profitable one, around your moonlighting job.

If you prefer the security and regular income of working for someone else, then chances are you have already decided on a moonlighting job in this category. Thus, you've already got your foot in the door. You're in an ideal position to examine the prospects for future pay and advancement that your moonlighting job affords. Compare these prospects with your present full-time job, if it's in a different field, and make your choice. You have the advantage of knowing right when an opening comes up on your part-time job, and you're right on the spot.

On the other hand, if moonlighting has attracted you to some independent endeavor, where you are your own boss at least on a part-time basis, you may be on the verge of discovering a whole new world of employment—working for yourself.

This chapter could change your life, once you realize how simple it is to set yourself up in business, how thrilling it is to see your own name on a company letterhead, and how profitable it can be.

Do you think you couldn't possibly afford to go into business for yourself? Nonsense! Here is one startling fact that may quickly change your thinking: Going into business for yourself can require less than a twenty dollar bill! That's all it takes to march down to a printer and order letterhead stationery and business cards. Aside from this expense, all you need is a telephone, and you can start out with your own home phone or an answering service.

Suppose you have been moonlighting in typewriter repairs. Ask a printer to prepare cards and letterheads listing your service, your name, address, and telephone number; he'll help you word it right. If you usually are not home during business hours because of your present job, your spouse or someone else can answer the telephone inquiries and promise you'll call back. Whoever answers the phone should use your business name, or just answer with the telephone number, until it is determined whether the call is business or personal. Or an answering service is a good small investment to make sure you sound businesslike and don't miss an important customer call. Many answering services will also let you use their address for mail if you wish, and the charge is often as small as $5 a month.

If you need working space until your operation has grown large enough to rent a store or office, how about your basement, a spare room, or even your attic or garage? Or if impressing customers is important, you can inquire at small office buildings where sometimes they have switchboard answering service for all calls, and single desk space at a very low rent. Now, hang up a sign and you're in business! That's how easy it is.

Think about it. You set your own hours, you collect all the profits, and you answer to no orders except your own. You own your own company, however small; you're an independent businessman.

Consider this: if you happen to be a plumber or other skilled tradesman, but have been working for a company at an hourly rate, all you need to strike off on your own are the tools, the customers, and the guts. And, if you've tried it on a moonlighting basis, you've already learned that the pay you collect is a lot higher than your hourly wage.

Those with a special skill—blue collar, white collar or whatever —will find the transition easy once they've read this chapter. The bookkeeper, the secretary, the cabinet maker, the ceramic artist can take his first step safely, on a part-time basis, exploring the possibilities gradually. Print up business cards and pass them out to prospects, then sit back and watch the inquiries come in. When there are enough of them, you've got your own clientele; you can quit your job and go into business for yourself. One tip on this: it's best not to solicit business from your current boss' customers; not right now, anyway. Just make a list of names and addresses and when you are on your own, then it's fair play to send your card to those people who already know your work, to tell them you're available.

You needn't have a long-apprenticed trade or skill to make the big switch from worker to self-employed. A janitor who calls on office building managers and offers them nightly cleanup is on the verge of starting his own business, and now he's no longer a janitor; he's a building maintenance specialist. A widow who expands a back yard henhouse has multiplied herself into the poultry and egg farming business. A young man with a camera who has discovered a market for his pictures has become a professional photographer. A housewife who stitches native dolls and markets them through a local souvenir store has become a manufacturer.

A product or service to sell, and the customers—that's all it takes. And the beauty of moonlighting is that you can test the whole market prospect while hanging on to the security of a regular job. The approach you've got to take, if you'd like to sample the career prospects of your moonlighting job, is to start treating the part-time venture as though you already were taking the plunge into independent business.

Whether you are running the business full or part time, whether you are an electrician or deliveryman, a maker of a specialty product, or the selling of a common, everyday item, there are several points to be examined carefully:

(1)   What about my prices? Can a customer buy the product or service cheaper elsewhere? Am I selling bargains or quality? Are my customers' incomes high enough that quality is most important?

(2)   How do I compare with the competition? If my prices are competitive, do I offer faster service? A better job? More attractive packaging? Variety? Thoroughness?

(3)   What selling techniques should I use? A sign by the roadside or an ad in a national magazine? When I sell a product or service, do I overlook the chance to recommend further business?

(4)   What special service will I feature? Credit buying? Free delivery? Guaranteed satisfaction? Repair service? Free estimates?

(5)   How do I make myself available to the public? Is my telephone always answered in a businesslike way? Do I return calls promptly on inquiries?

(6)   Who are my customers? Homeowners? Travelers? Men?

Women? Teenagers? Where are they located? How do I reach them to tell them about my product or service?

The answer to the latter point is, of course, advertising, the keystone to successful business today. And that holds true even for the highly specialized product or service which never is promoted in a single line of newspaper advertising, direct mail, or even a sign, because the best advertising of all can be simple referrals, the word-of-mouth advertising in which one customer tells a neighbor or friend who it is who does such a good job with the gardening, or where it was that he bought such a beautiful piece of jewelry.

How much advertising you do can well determine the success or failure of any business venture. An accountant, for example, may do his best advertising by calling on small business managers and giving them his business card with the suggestion that he might be of service once a week, once a month, or just at tax time. But a small, periodic ad in the Services Offered column of the local newspaper classified section might bring in additional business. And, of course, the Yellow Pages gives the image of permanence, reliability, and availability. On the other hand, compiling a list of all prospective employers or customers, from that same telephone book, and contacting them directly by mail, telephone, or in person could be the key to independent success. The basic message is this: "Hello, I'm John Doe, experienced accountant, and I'm willing and able to do your books for you on a part-time basis."

How much advertising the newcomer to business does will depend on how many people he must get his message to, and the best method of reaching them.

Being new to a retail or service business, you may learn about advertising through trial and error. Watch your competitors, the successful ones. A newcomer should always keep one question foremost in mind: how much good is my advertising doing? You don't have to engage in complicated ad measurement methods, but you can use certain rule-of-thumb devices to get a better idea than you may now have about the results of your advertising.

There are two basic approaches to advertising:

(1) *Immediate response advertising* is designed to cause potential customers to buy a particular product or service from you within a short time—today, tomorrow, the weekend, or next week. An example of such decision-triggering ads is one that promotes price appeal.

Such advertising should be checked daily for results or at the end of one week from appearance.

(2)   *Attitude advertising* is the type you use to keep your name before the public. Some people think of this type as "image-building" advertising. With it, you remind people week after week about your merchandise or services or tell them about new or special services or policies. It is your reputation builder. To some degree, all advertising should be attitude advertising. The same rules apply whether your advertising is limited to the Yellow Pages, the want ads, business cards, or display ads in your community newspaper. Don't be afraid to ask customers who recommended you.

Plan ads so they will make you stand out consistently when people read or hear about your product or service. Identify it fully and clearly. Give your address and telephone number. Make copy easy to read. Try different wordings until you find the combination that brings the best response. Vary the offer from week to week and watch the results.

When advertising is spread out over a selling season or several seasons, part of the measurement job is keeping records. Your aim is comparing records of ads and sales for an extended time. An easy way to set up a file is by marking the date of appearance on tear sheets of newspaper ads, log reports of radio and television ads, and copies of direct mail ads. The file may be broken down into monthly, quarterly, or semi-annual blocks. By recording the sales of the advertised items on each ad or log, you can make comparisons.

Although many factors influence customer's decisions on where they buy, reputation is a big one. Customers place the "image" which a store or service creates high on their list because they like to be a part of success.

They want no part of failure. When a company reflects an image that is out of step with the times, most people don't like to be seen shopping there. A service that evokes a fly-by-night image is ignored.

On the other hand, if you and your firm have a reputation for being in step with progress, offering up-to-the-minute products and services in an exciting way, people will boast about buying from you or hiring you. This is the same kind of impulsive reasoning that makes some people pay hard cash for a label on a coat.

It's important to examine where customers buy, and the best way to do this is to put yourself in their shoes. Why do you buy your own suits, shirts, shoes and groceries in certain stores and not in others? Have you changed your buying habits recently and do you realize

why you switched from one store to another? If you have been going to the same stores and the same repairmen for a long time, what
is it that causes your loyalty to them? Thinking about these questions can help you run your business or service the way that will
make your customers keep coming back to you.

By taking an analytical look at yourself and your own buying habits you can learn a lot about your potential customers. The customer
you want is probably a person very little different from yourself.
Little things can cause a quick shift in his patronage from one place
to another. To please the customer, you have to get to know a little
bit about him. You'll never be able to divide customers into exact
categories, because every person is a little different, but whatever
you can learn about what kind of people they are can set your pattern for pleasing them. For example, if you are selling rock 'n roll
records, a store with the walls covered by psychedelic posters is
fine, but if your customers are conservative working people and
your product is reconditioned television sets, then a more sedate de-
cor is best.

Early in the preparations for setting up your business of service,
you should try to discover the kinds of people you will be serving,
or want to be serving, what they need and want, and how you can
make buying a pleasant experience for them.

People whose location, income, business, social status, age and
sex make them logical customers for your goods or service are the
ones to keep your eyes on, and the guiding factors should include
these six points:

(1)   What hours do they like to shop or what days or time of day do
they want a specific service done?

(2)   Do they like to pay cash, be billed later, use a credit card or
buy on time?

(3)   Do they tend to buy bargains or quality—in other words, is a
low price the biggest factor in bringing in a lot of customers, or is
top quality in products and workmanship the vital factor?

(4)   What type of stores or operators are getting the most business
from these people; what do these stores look like and how are they
arranged?

(5)   How old is the customer? Who does the actual buying—husband or wife, mother or son, newlyweds together, elderly men or
women?

(6)   What is their income level? What kind of homes do they live in and do your products and services suit the needs of such homes?

Your basic techniques may be decided by examining customers from those viewpoints. Other than trying to fill your customers' needs better than anyone else in your business is doing, don't overlook one of the best means of advertising and promotion—the customers themselves.

You can enlist, at no cost to yourself, a whole army of auxiliary salespeople: your customers. They are willing to help you sell things or services for several reasons, but the main reason is that they usually want to justify their own purchases. When they talk to others about the product or service they bought and the others decide to buy the same, then their judgment is reaffirmed. Oversimplified, the idea is this, a person has bought something he is pleased with; whatever words he uses, he is saying to others, "See how smart I am; see how much money I saved by buying this excellent thing." If people believe what he says, they can offer no better proof than rushing out and buying one themselves.

It's one of the key factors in business. Call it good will or anything else. The fact is, people like to share their discoveries—a good, honest auto mechanic or a reasonable plumber will find that most customers will enjoy passing on the benefits they have gained by dealing with them. People like to feel that they are helping others by recommending for or against certain products or services.

You realize how this can be such a vital factor when you consider that a special sale, with bargain prices as low as you can offer, can boomerang and hurt your business, actually losing more customers than you gain. Have you ever bought a major appliance, for example, for $225, being well pleased with your purchase for about two weeks. Then it happens. The store has a special sale and the same article you paid $225 for now is selling for $199! Wouldn't you be angry enough not to go back there again? Why couldn't the salesman have warned you that a big bargain sale was coming? Some retailers and businessmen solve this difficulty by a straightforward approach, such as sending all regular customers a bonus deduction on their next purchase, to make up for the sale price differential. Instead of angering customers with a sale, the tactic builds future business.

But to do this, a retailer or specialist in services must keep a list of regular customers and keep in touch with them through the mails. Even if a person pays all cash for every transaction, the good businessman will find a way to get his name and address for his mailing list. When you've got people like this working for you, on their own time, you can't afford to lose them. You can't afford an unhappy customer, whatever line you are in.

If you want to prove to yourself how valuable word-of-mouth advertising is, make a simple experiment: For the next ten days, write down in a little notebook all the things your friends recommend to you in casual conversation. At the end of that time, you will find that they have been trying to persuade you to go and see a certain motion picture, for example—one that they saw and liked. Film exhibitors have found that no matter how much they advertise, they can't attract a crowd unless people start telling each other how good the picture is. If the word-of-mouth verdict is bad, the customers just don't come.

Or maybe friends recommended a certain restaurant. If they praised the food and service, they'll go back, and if you try it and like it, you'll return, too.

If a neighbor of yours is excited about his new car, he's probably been showing it off to you in a way that says, "You ought to get a car like mine."

Housewives are especially prone to this one—household items. If a neighbor or friend just bought a handy kitchen tool or a lovely piece of furnishing, it immediately creates the demand that she have one, too. And it isn't just a matter of keeping up with the Joneses.

Analyze each suggestion that was made to you. Maybe some of the people were trying to convince themselves that they did indeed get a good buy, or just that they weren't "taken." Was it a matter of bragging, a case of trying to impress you with how smart a shopper they were? Whatever the personality, you will find that there were two ingredients in each recommendation; there was a certain level of enthusiasm, and a certain amount of honesty. What would any acquaintance gain, except a possible punch in the nose, by misrepresenting the deal he got if it were a bad one? Why would he bring it up at all?

Once you recognize the workings of such advertising, like an endless chain letter, you will find that it can be applied to any type of business. The approach you take is this: give them a little something to talk about.

For example, an electrician who goes into homes to repair or install wiring makes it a regular practice to replace the living room main light switches with better ones. They cost him $.50 and a few minutes, but every time they are used they remind the customer of the extra value given gratis. A house painter always leaves his customers a small amount of their shade of paint for possible future touch-ups, a little gesture that costs nothing and earns a lot of good will. A nurseryman includes in his monthly bills to his customers little brochures, printed by distributors, telling about the care of grass, shrubs, and trees. Sometimes he mails out packets of flower seeds stamped with his company name. The seeds cost him a few cents, but when they are planted they are a constant reminder of the something extra his customers get; and even if the customer can't use the seeds, he has the opportunity to give them away to a friend or neighbor, so what could be better advertising?

The examples are endless: a clothing store supplies a little envelope with spare buttons or a coil of thread for future repairs; a fruit stand gives away a free newspaper in each basket of fruit sold; a motel offers free continental breakfast of coffee, juice, and roll; a forward-looking jeweler offers credit cards to teenagers, creating a whole force of future customers who will graduate from friendship rings and cufflinks in school days into engagement ring buyers a few years from now.

Little extra touches like this are the secret of success in dealing with people. They will return again and again to the stores and services which treat their customers to extra value.

Did you know that research has proven that people who already own a certain product will read advertisements about that product more thoroughly than those who do not own it? It is the same principle at work—the customer reassuring himself of the good deal he got, comparing the ads to reaffirm his judgment and satisfaction.

A word or two about cash and books: even the smallest retail and service companies or individual operators should keep records which will show them whether they are making a big enough profit from their work. If you don't keep a simple set of books, how will you know if, perhaps, you are actually selling your product or service too cheaply? And—this is very important—if you come to a point where a bank loan could mean the difference between expansion or failure, you'll need some businesslike records to show the lender that you've got a going thing, be it part time or full time.

You don't need elaborate ledgers which require hours of detail work every day. A few minutes a day can take care of the book work for you, so long as you make it a rule to follow a regular set of rules. Here are key tips which, if followed, will help you in the black:

(1)   Always handle your business cash as though you were working for somebody else. Never mix together your personal money and your business income, even if you have to pay yourself a regular salary. Separation is a must.

(2)   Keep regular entries showing all incoming cash—just a simple note stating the amount, the date, and the source.

(3)   Use a separate bank account for your business money, and a separate bank checking account from your personal one; deposit all cash receipts in this account, daily.

(4)   Never make a payment for anything out of cash receipts; pay all business bills by check so that you have a record.

(5)   Set up a petty cash fund for small, out-of-pocket business expenses such as postage, pencils, paper. Balance the account regularly so you have a record of each penny.

(6)   Keep your records simple enough to cover the necessities and still be readable. The easier it is to glance at and gain information from your records, the more help they'll be.

(7)   Review your records regularly.

If you follow those simple rules, you will have the kind of book control you need. You will be able to look for trouble spots and correct them before it is too late. What to look for? Well, after a few weeks, or months of record keeping, you should be able to add up a few figures and determine:

(1)   Were expenses greater than the gross profit you made from your sales or services?

(2)   Was there enough cash on hand for expenses at the start of each month?

(3)   If the business bank balance is low, are there too many accounts receivable—that means customers who haven't paid you yet —enough for you to send out little reminders? Nice ones, though, you don't want to lose customers.

Sometimes banks will lend money on accounts receivable, which are considered an asset. If new equipment or some expansion is called for to increase income, perhaps a short-term loan is what you need. Especially if there are seasonal fluctuations in your business.

Many small businessmen, whether in retail or service operations, borrow money from the bank several times a year when their deposit gets small and some expense is coming up. If you are maintaining a regular business bank account, the bank looks favorable on such lending. It can be advantageous to you, for example, in cases where a 10 per cent discount is offered to you for payment of bills for supplies, if you pay within thirty days. Borrow the money at less than 10 per cent and it's a gain. Little tricks like this can add up to the difference between profit and loss.

The key ingredients to profit, which should be evident in the records you keep, are costs, selling price, and volume of sales. All factors must be present in a business operation in the proper proportion or something is wrong. Everybody has heard auto dealers broadcasting that they deal in volume sales, so they are able practically to give their cars away. Nonsense. Volume alone does not mean profit to any business. Grocery stores often advertise one or two articles for sale at a loss or break-even price to bring in crowds. But if they did that with all their goods, the big volume of sales would only put them further and further in the red.

You have to understand several factors to establish the best prices for your products or service, because no one rule applies in all situations. Again a key point is knowing your customers. For example, suppose you are a cabinet maker. A supplier offers to sell you lumber or hardware you need at a lower price, but it is of a lower quality than you have been using. With the savings, you could lower your prices and attract more customers, it would seem. But what if your customers care more about quality than price? In the latter case, you would be better off buying more expensive supplies and increasing your prices!

Four considerations are important in fixing your prices: your direct costs, such as supplies; your labor and the labor of others who must be compensated; overhead such as office or store space, depreciation on tools and equipment, and selling costs; plus profit. Balance them all with the one overriding viewpoint; what is best for my customers, including potential ones, considering current market conditions, and you'll come up with your price.

Weighing costs and profits again stresses the importance of keeping adequate records, even if you are working on your business or service on a part-time basis. For example, suppose you have been employed full time at a factory but have been slowly building up a sideline, say a landscaping service, on a moonlighting basis. Now there comes a time when you've built up so many satisfied customers that you have to make a choice: either stop building up the landscaping business or quit the factory and go at it whole hog.

But you can't quite afford the plunge. Maybe you'd need a new truck, new tools, a helper. Or maybe there's an opportunity to buy into a landscaping and nursery outfit, if you only had the cash. If you've kept a good set of records that can prove the success and growth of your venture, chances are you can borrow the money and take the plunge.

Being able to get the money you need, when you need it, is an important asset to the security of any business. If you know in advance what kind of people the bank lending officer is eager to lend money too, you've got the answers ready to all the questions he'll ask before putting the "OK" stamp on your loan application. What he'll want to know is this:

(1)   Character is most important of all—your credit record, what kind of person you are, your attitudes, your business ability.

(2)   What are you going to do with the money, specifically? Depending on whether you are investing in supplies or products for quick resale, or buying long-lasting equipment that will be a business asset, the decision will be made as to whether the loan is short term or long term.

(3)   What plans do you have for paying the loan off? Can you show the banker a few projected figures which will illustrate enough future income to put you in a position to repay the loan?

(4)   What about a cushion? Bankers often insist that a business applicant take more than he requested to make allowance for unforeseen developments. Is the loan large enough?

(5)   How is business in general in your town, and especially the kind of business you are entering?

Most bankers today recognize that they need good borrowers as much or more than the borrowers need them, and the stigma of a loan being a handout has vanished from the face of American business to the extent that it is considered very good business practice to use as much of somebody else's money—not your own—as you can, in the process of making more money for yourself. But when you set out to the bank, you should know a few things about the kinds of loan available; short-term money, term money, and equity capital. Which do you need?

The planned use of the money and the repayment source usually decide for you. There are both secured and unsecured loans, and the difference between them is collateral. For a secured loan you pledge a part or all of your assets as a guarantee of repayment, while an unsecured loan merely relies on your credit reputation. Short-term loans usually are unsecured.

For a loan from thirty days to six months, you are in the short-term category. Maybe it's for a bargain winter purchase of air conditioners that will sell for twice the price in the summer, or maybe it's just to hold out until customers start paying the bills they owe you.

Term borrowing is dealing in sums you wish to repay over a longer period of time—one year to five or more. Usually the loan is sought for equipment which will be used to make profit, and the sum is to be repaid out of the earnings. The equipment serves as collateral.

Equity capital is the same as investment money, it doesn't have to be repaid. You sell a part of your business, a share of the profits in exchange for the sum of money you need. You are taking a partner who risks the same as you and gets the same rewards.

When you go to the bank for a loan, a budget and business forecast for a period of time up to a year can help you get your loan without a hitch. It's not as difficult as it seems. Suppose you have been working part time at your business, nights and weekends for six months, averaging twelve hours a week. Well, since you are planning to go into it full time, you can figure out your costs and profits on a per-hour basis and multiply by forty or forty-eight, allowing for seasonal dips, for your weekly cost and profit once you are built up to full time. Estimate how long it will take to get enough business for full-week figures, and space the income projection out from the current twelve hours to the planned forty hours. Your banker will recognize honest projections, with a conservative allowance for anticipated ups and downs.

Well, if you've got the idea, the skill, the inclination, and the money you need to go into business, there's little else to consider, so let's go.

There may be city or county regulations which require you to take out a business license and pay a business tax, but don't let the prospect of red tape discourage you. A visit or telephone call to your city or county clerk will give you all the information you need. Sometimes, depending on the type of business you are about to engage in, a simple registration form is all that is required.

Later, when things start expanding, you might want to consider the advantages of incorporating. Laws governing the procedure for obtaining a corporate charter vary with the individual state. Details generally are available either from the office of the Secretary of

State or from your state's special corporation official. If and when you get to this step, consult a lawyer and discuss with him the advantages and disadvantages of the move.

All you'll need to start with is a business certificate or license from your local governing agency, and in some small operations, even this is not necessary. In the case of businesses where food or child care is involved, the Health Department should be consulted, and in the building trades, your local Building and Safety Department.

For advice on the business picture in your locality, a trade association in the field you are concerned with can be a valuable source of information. They may have statistics that will really open your eyes on business prospects in your area, and they'll be familiar with all the short-cuts and problems you'll face in starting out.

Another valuable source of help, the United States Government's Small Business Administration, may have a regional office near you. The SBA publishes the following checklist of questions to consider for anyone going into business for himself:

(1) Have you rated your personal traits such as leadership, organizing ability, perseverance, and physical energy?

(2) Have you had some friends rate you on them?

(3) Have you considered getting an associate whose strong points will compensate for your weak traits?

(4) Have you had any actual business experience?

(5) Do you have special technical skills, such as those needed by plumber, electrician, mechanic, or radio repairman?

(6) Have you obtained some basic management experience working for someone else?

(7) Have you analyzed the recent trend of business conditions (good or bad)?

(8) Have you analyzed business conditions in the city and neighborhood where you want to locate?

(9) Have you analyzed conditions in the line of business you are planning?

(10) Have you determined what size business you plan to establish (dollar sales per year)?

(11) Have you built up a detailed set of figures on how much capital you will need to launch the business?

(12)   Have you figured how much time you will need until the business income equals the expenses?

(13)   Have you planned what net profit you believe you should make?

(14)   Will the net profit divided by the investment result in a rate of return which compares favorably with the rate you can obtain from other investment opportunities?

(15)   Have you worked out what income from sales or services you can reasonably expect in the first six months? The first year?

(16)   Do you know what net profit you can expect on these volumes?

(17)   Have you made a conservative forecast of expenses, including a regular salary for yourself?

(18)   Have you compared this income with what you could make working for someone else?

(19)   Are you willing to risk uncertain or irregular income for the next year?

(20)   Have you counted up how much actual money you have to invest in your business?

(21)   Do you have other assets which you could sell or on which you could borrow?

(22)   Have you some other source from which you could borrow money?

(23)   Have you talked to a banker?

(24)   Is he favorably impressed with your plan?

(25)   Do you have a financial reserve for unexpected needs?

(26)   Does your total capital, from all cources, cover your best estimates of the capital you will need?

Don't let the formidable list scare you. If you've got the initiative to set out on your own, and self-confidence in your idea for business success, you have the basic qualifications. And from there, the sky's the limit.

EASY JOB GUIDE

U. Bellugi & R. Brown (Eds.), The acquisition of language. *Monographs of the Society for Research in Child Development, 92*(29), 79–92.

Bruininks, R.H., Woodcock, R.W., Weatherman, R.F., & Hill, B.K. (1984). *Scales of Independent Behavior, Woodcock-Johnson Psychoeducational Battery: Part Four.* Allen, TX: Developmental Learning Materials.

Campbell, P. (1983). Basic considerations in programming for students with movement difficulties. In M.E. Snell (Ed.), *Systematic instruction of the moderately and severely handicapped* (pp. 168–202). Columbus, OH: Charles E. Merrill.

Campbell, P.H. (1987). The integrated programming team: An approach for coordinating professionals of various disciplines in programs for students with severe and multiple handicaps. *Journal of The Association for Persons with Severe Handicaps, 12,* 107–116.

Carrow-Woolfolk, E., & Lynch, J.I. (1982). *An integrative approach to language disorders in children.* New York: Grune & Stratton.

Certo, N. (1983). Characteristics of educational services. In M.E. Snell (Ed.), *Systematic instruction of the moderately and severely handicapped* (pp. 2–15). Columbus, OH: Charles E. Merrill

Cole, M.L., & Cole, J.T. (1981). *Effective intervention with the language impaired child.* Rockville, MD: Aspen Systems.

Comas-Diaz, L., & Griffith, E.H. (1988). *Clinical guidelines in cross-cultural mental health.* New York: John Wiley & Sons.

Cone, J.D. (1984). *The Pyramid Scales: Criterion-referenced measures of adaptive behavior in severely handicapped persons.* Austin, TX: PRO-ED.

Cossairt, A., Hall, R.V., & Hopkins, B.L. (1973). The effects of experimenter's instructions, feedback, and praise on teacher praise and student attending behavior. *Journal of Applied Behavior Analysis, 6,* 89–100.

Craighead, W.E., Mercatoris, M., & Bellack, B. (1974). A brief report on mentally retarded residents as behavioral observers. *Journal of Applied Behavior Analysis, 7,* 333–340.

Crist, K., Walls, R.T., & Haught, P. (1984). Degree of specificity in task analysis. *American Journal of Mental Deficiency, 89,* 67–74.

Cronin, K.A., & Cuvo, A.J. (1979). Teaching mending skills to retarded adolescents. *Journal of Applied Behavior Analysis, 12,* 401–406.

Csapo, M. (1981). Evaluation of the teaching effectiveness of special education teachers-in-training. *Teacher Education and Special Education, 4,* 21–30.

Cuvo, A.J. (1978). Validating task analysis of community living skills. *Vocational Evaluation and Work Adjustment Bulletin, 11*(3), 13–21.

Cuvo, A.J., Jacobi, E., & Sipko, R. (1981). Teaching laundry skills to mentally retarded students. *Education and Training of the Mentally Retarded, 11,* 54–64.

Cuvo, A.J., Leaf, R.B., & Borakove, L.S. (1978). Teaching janitorial skills to the mentally retarded: Acquisition, generalization and maintenance. *Journal of Applied Behavior Analysis, 11,* 345-355.

Dattilo, J., & Mirenda, P. (1987). An application of a leisure preference assessment protocol for persons with severe handicaps. *Journal of The Association for Persons with Severe Handicaps, 12,* 306–311.

Demchak, M.A. (1987). A review of behavioral staff training in special education settings. *Education and Training in Mental Retardation, 22,* 205–217.

Demchak, M.A. (1990). Response prompting and fading methods: A review. *American Journal on Mental Retardation, 94,* 603–615.

Demchak, M.A., & Browder, D.M. (1987). Data-based teacher supervision: Evaluation task analytic instruction. *Journal of Special Education Technology, 9,* 9–18.

Demchak, M.A., & Koury, M. (1990). Differential reinforcement of leisure activities: An observation form for supervisors. *Teaching Exceptional Children, 22*(2), 14–17.

Deno, S.L. (1985). Curriculum-based measurement. The emerging alternative. *Exceptional Children, 52*(3), 219–232.

Deno, S.L., & Mirkin, P.K. (1977). *Data-based program modification: A manual.* Reston, VA: Council for Exceptional Children.

DeProspero, A., & Cohen, S. (1979). Inconsistent visual analysis of intrasubject data. *Journal of Applied Behavior Analysis, 12,* 573–579.

Dever, R.B. (1988). *Community living skills: A taxonomy.* Washington, DC: American Association on Mental Retardation.

Donnellan, A.M. (1984). The criterion of the least dangerous assumption. *Behavioral Disorders: Journal of the Council for Children with Behavioral Disorders, 9*(2), 141–150.

Donnellan, A., Mirenda, P., Mesaros, R., & Fassbender, L. (1984). Analyzing the communicative functions of aberrant behavior. *Journal of The Association for Persons with Severe Handicaps, 9,* 201–212.

Duncan, D., Sbardellati, E., Maheady, L., & Sainato, D. (1981). Nondiscriminatory assessment of severely physically handicapped individuals. *Journal of The Association of the Severely Handicapped, 6*(2), 17–22.

Dunlap, G. (1984). The influence of task variation and maintenance tasks on the learning and affect of autistic children. *Journal of Experimental Child Psychology, 37,* 41–64.

Dunst, C.J. (1980). *A clinical and educational manual for use with the Uzgiris and Hunt Scales of Infant Psychological Development.* Baltimore: University Park Press.

Durand, M.M. (1982). Analysis and intervention of self-injurious behavior. *Journal of The Association for the Severely Handicapped, 7*(4), 44–53.

Durand, M. (1990). *Severe behavior problems. A functional communication training program.* New York: Guilford Press.

Dyer, K., Schwartz, I., & Luce, S. (1984). A supervisory program for increasing functional activities for severely handicapped students in a residential setting. *Journal of Applied Behavior Analysis, 17,* 249–259.

Elliott, S.N. (1985). AAMD Adaptive Behavior Scale. In O.K. Buros (Ed.), *Ninth mental measurements yearbook* (p. 3). Highland Park, NJ: Gryphon Press.

Eshilian, L., Haney, M., & Falvey, M.A. (1989). Domestic skills. In M.A. Falvey (Ed.), *Community-based curriculum: Instructional strategies for students with severe handicaps* (2nd ed., pp. 115–140). Baltimore: Paul H. Brookes Publishing Co.

Evans, L.D., & Bradley-Johnson, S. (1988). A review of recently developed measures of adaptive behavior. *Psychology in the Schools, 25,* 276–287.

Evans, I.M., & Meyer, L.H. (1985). *An educative approach to behavior problems: A practical decision model for interventions with severely handicapped learners.* Baltimore: Paul H. Brookes Publishing Co.

Falvey, M.A. (1986). *Community-based curriculum: Instructional strategies for students with severe handicaps.* Baltimore: Paul H. Brookes Publishing Co.

Falvey, M.A. (1989). *Community-based curriculum: Instructional strategies for students with severe handicaps* (2nd ed.). Baltimore: Paul H. Brookes Publishing Co.

Falvey, M., Brown, L., Lyon, S., Baumgart, D., & Schroeder, J. (1980). Strategies for using cues and correction procedures. In W. Sailor, B. Wilcox, & L. Brown (Eds.), *Methods of instruction for severely handicapped students* (pp. 109–133). Baltimore: Paul H. Brookes Publishing Co.

Farlow, L.J., & Snell, M.E. (1989). Teacher use of student performance data to make instructional decisions: Practices in programs for students with moderate to profound disabilities. *Journal of The Association for Persons with Severe Handicaps, 14,* 13–22.

Fixsen, D.L., Phillips, E.L., & Wolf, M.N. (1972). Achievement place: The reliability of self reporting and peer reporting and their effects on behavior. *Journal of Applied Behavior Analysis, 5,* 19–30.

Ford, A., Schnorr, R., Meyer, L., Davern, L., Black, J., & Dempsey, P. (1989a). General community functioning. In A. Ford, R. Schnorr, L. Meyer, L. Davern, J. Black, & P. Dempsey (Eds.), *The Syracuse community-referenced curriculum guide for students with moderate and severe disabilities* (pp. 77–92). Baltimore: Paul H. Brookes Publishing Co.

Ford, A., Schnorr, R., Meyer, L., Davern, L., Black, J., & Dempsey, P. (Eds.). (1989b). *The Syracuse community-referenced curriculum guide for students with moderate and severe disabilities.* Baltimore: Paul H. Brookes Publishing Co.

Forest, M., & Pearpoint, J. (1990). Supports for addressing severe maladaptive behaviors. In W. Stainback & S. Stainback (Eds.), *Support networks for inclusive schooling: Interdependent integrated education* (pp. 187–197). Baltimore: Paul H. Brookes Publishing Co.

Frankenburg, W.K., Dodds, J.B., & Frandal, A.W. (1968–70). *Denver Developmental Screening Test.* Denver: Ladoca Project and Publishing Foundation.

Fraser, B.A., & Hensinger, R.N. (1983). *Managing physical handicaps: A practical guide for parents, care providers, and educators.* Baltimore: Paul H. Brookes Publishing Co.

Fredericks, H.D., Anderson, R., & Baldwin, V. (1979) The identification of compentency indicators of teachers of the severely handicapped. *AAESPH Review, 4,* 81–95.

Fuchs, L.S., & Fuchs, D. (1986). Effects of systematic formative evaluation: A meta-analysis. *Exceptional Children, 53,* 199–208.

Gaylord-Ross, R.J. (1979). Mental retardation research, ecological validity, and the delivery of longitudinal education programs. *Journal of Special Education, 13,* 69–80.

Gaylord-Ross, R. (1980). A decision model for the treatment of aberrant behavior in applied settings. In W. Sailor, B. Wilcox, & L. Brown (Eds.), *Methods of instruction for severely handicapped students* (pp. 135–158). Baltimore: Paul H. Brookes Publishing Co.

Gaylord-Ross, R., & Browder, D. (1990). Functional assessment: Dynamic and domain properties. In L.H. Meyer, C.A. Peck, & L. Brown (Eds.), *Critical issues in the lives of people with severe disabilities* (pp. 45–66). Baltimore: Paul H. Brookes Publishing Co.

Gaylord-Ross, R., & Holvoet, J. (1985). *Strategies for educating students with severe handicaps.* Boston: Little, Brown.

Geiger, W.L., & Justen, J.E. (1983). Definitions of *severely handicapped* and requirements for teacher certification: A survey of state departments of education. *Journal of The Association for the Severely Handicapped, 8*(1), 25–29.

Georgia Association of Retarded Citizens v. McDaniel. Civ. A. No. C-78-1950A. (N.D. Georgia, 1979).

Gilbreth, F.B., & Gilbreth, L.M. (1917). *Applied motion study.* New York: Sturgis & Walton.

Goetz, L., Guess, D., & Stremel-Campbell, K. (Eds.). (1987). *Innovative program design for individuals with dual sensory impairments.* Baltimore: Paul H. Brookes Publishing Co.

Greene, B.F., Willis, B.S., Levy, R., & Bailey, J.S. (1978). Measuring client gains from staff-implemented programs. *Journal of Applied Behavior Analysis, 11,* 395–412.

Greenspan, S., & Shoultz, B. (1981). Why mentally retarded adults lose their jobs: Social competence as a factor in work adjustment. *Applied Research in Mental Retardation, 2,* 23–38.

Grigg, N.C., Snell, M.E., & Lloyd, B. (1989). Visual analysis of student evaluation data: A qualitative analysis of teacher decision making. *Journal of The Association for Persons with Severe Handicaps, 14,* 23–32.

Guess, D., Horner, D., Utley, B., Holvoet, J., Maxon, D., Tucker, D., & Warren, S. (1978). A functional curriculum sequencing model for teaching the severely handicapped. *AAESPH Review, 8*(3), 202–215.

Halderman v. Pennhurst State School and Hospital, 446 F. Supp. 1295 (E.D. Pa. 1977).

Hammill, D.D., & Larsen, S.C. (1974). The effectiveness of psycholinguistic training. *Exceptional Children, 40,* 5–12.

Handleman, J., Powers, M., & Harris, S. (1981). *The teaching of labels to autistic children.* Paper presented to the American Association of Behavior Therapy, Toronto.

Hanley-Maxwell, C., Rusch, F.R., Chadsey-Rusch, J., & Renzaglia, A. (1986). Reported factors contributing to job terminations of individuals with severe disabilities. *Journal of The Association for Persons with Severe Handicaps, 11,* 45–52.

Haring, N., Liberty, K., & White, O. (1979). *Handbook of experimental procedures.* Seattle: University of Washington, Instructional Hierarchies Research Project.

Haring, N., Liberty, K., & White, O. (1980). Rules for data-based strategy decisions in instructional programs: Current research and instructional implications. In W. Sailor, B. Wilcox, & L. Brown (Eds.), *Methods of instruction for severely handicapped learners* (pp. 159–192). Baltimore: Paul H. Brookes Publishing Co.

Haring, N., Liberty, K., & White, O. (1981). *An investigation of phases of learning and facilitating instructional events for the severely/profoundly handicapped* (Final project report). Seattle: University of Washington.

Haring, T.G., & Kennedy, C.H. (1988). Units of analysis in task-analytic research. *Journal of Applied Behavior Analysis, 21,* 207–215.

Hersen, M., & Barlow, D. (1976). *Single-case experimental designs: Strategies for studying behavior change.* Elmsford, NY: Pergamon Press.

Holvoet, J., Guess, D., Mulligan, M., & Brown, F. (1980). The individualized curriculum sequencing model. (II): A teaching strategy for severely handicapped students. *Journal of The Association for the Severely Handicapped, 5,* 325–336.

Holvoet, J., O'Neil, C., Chazdon, L., Carr, D., & Warner, J. (1983). Hey, do we really have to take data? *Journal of The Association for the Severely Handicapped, 5,* 56–70.

Horner, R.H., McDonnell, J.J., & Bellamy, G.T. (1986). Teaching generalized skills: General case instruction in simulation and community settings. In R.H. Horner, L.H. Meyer, & H.D.B. Fredericks (Eds.), *Education of learners with severe handicaps: Exemplary service strategies* (pp. 289–314). Baltimore: Paul H. Brookes Publishing Co.

Horner, R.H., Meyer, L.H., & Fredericks, H.D.B. (Eds.). (1986). *Education of learners with severe handicaps: Exemplary service strategies.* Baltimore: Paul H. Brookes Publishing Co.

Horner, R.H., Sprague, J., & Wilcox, B. (1982). General case programming for community activities. In B. Wilcox & G.T. Bellamy (Eds.), *Design of high school programs for severely handicapped students* (pp. 61–98). Baltimore: Paul H. Brookes Publishing Co.

Hunt, P., Goetz, L., & Anderson, J. (1986). The quality of IEP objectives associated with placement on integrated versus segregated school sites. *Journal of The Association for Persons with Severe Handicaps, 11,* 125–130.

Hutchison, J.M., Jarman, P.H., & Bailey, J.S. (1980). Public posting with a habilitation team: Effects on attendance and performance. *Behavior Modification, 4,* 57–70.

Inge, K.J., & Snell, M.E. (1985). Teaching positioning and handling techniques to public school personnel through inservice training. *Journal of The Association for Persons with Severe Handicaps, 10,* 105–110.

Ipsen, S.M. (1986). Test review: Scales of independent behavior: Woodcock-Johnson Psycho-Educational Battery, part four. *Education and Training of the Mentally Retarded, 21*, 153–154.

Iwata, B.A., Dorsey, M.F., Slifer, K.J., Bauman, K.E., & Richman, G.S. (1982). Toward a functional analysis of self injury. *Analysis and Intervention in Developmental Disabilities, 3*, 3–20.

Johnson, B.F., & Cuvo, A.J. (1981). Teaching mentally retarded adults to cook. *Behavior Modifications, 5*, 187–202.

Kahn, J.V. (1978). Acceleration of object permanence with severely and profoundly retarded children. *AAESPH Review, 3*, 15–22.

Kayser, J.E., Billingsley, F.F., & Neel, R.S. (1986). A comparison of in-context and traditional instructional approaches: Total task, single trial versus backward chaining, multiple trials. *Journal of The Association for Persons with Severe Handicaps, 11*, 28–38.

Kayser, J.E., Rallo, P., Rockwell, G., Aillaud, W., & Hu, F. (1986). Review of IEPs. In W.J. Schill (principal investigator), *Institute for Transition Research on Problems of Handicapped, annual report, 1985–86*. Washington, DC: U.S. Department of Education.

Kazdin, A.E. (1977). Assessing the clinical or applied importance of behavior change through social validation. *Behavior Modification, 1*, 472–452.

Kazdin, A.E. (1980). *Behavior modification in applied settings* (2nd ed.). Homewood, IL: Dorsey Press.

Kazdin, A.E. (1982). *Single-case research design*. New York: Oxford University Press.

Keogh, W.J., & Reichle, J. (1985). Communication intervention for the "difficult-to-teach" severely handicapped. In S.F. Warren & A.K. Rogers-Warren (Eds.), *Teaching functional language: Generalization and maintenance of language skill* (pp. 157–196). Baltimore: University Park Press.

Kirk, S., McCarthy, J., & Kirk, W. (1968). *Illinois Test of Psycholinguistic Abilities*. Urbana: University of Illinois Press.

Kishi, G., Teelucksingh, B., Zollers, N., Park-Lee, S., & Meyer, L. (1988). Daily decision making in community residences: A social comparison of adults with and without mental retardation. *American Journal on Mental Retardation, 92*, 430–435.

Kissel, R.C., Whitman, T.L., & Reid, D.H. (1983). An institutional staff training and self-management program for developing multiple self care skills in severely profoundly retarded individuals. *Journal of Applied Behavior Analysis, 16*, 395–415.

Koegel, L.K., & Koegel, R.L. (1986). The effects of interspersed maintenance tasks on academic performance in a severe childhood stroke victim. *Journal of Applied Behavior Analysis, 19*, 425–430.

Koegel, R.L., & Koegel, L.K. (1988). Generalized responsibility and pivotal behaviors. In R.H. Horner, G. Dunlap, & R.L. Koegel (Eds.), *Generalization and maintenance: Life-style changes in applied settings* (pp. 41–66). Baltimore: Paul H. Brookes Publishing Co.

Koegel, R.L., O'Dell, M.C., & Koegel, L.K. (1987). A natural language teaching paradigm for nonverbal autistic children. *Journal of Autism and Developmental Disorders, 17*, 187–200.

Koegel, R., Rincover, A., & Egel, A. (1982). *Educating and understanding autistic children*. San Diego: College-Hill Press.

Koegel, R., Russo, D.C., & Rincover, A. (1977). Assessing and training teachers in the generalized use of behavior modification with autistic children. *Journal of Applied Behavior Analysis, 10*, 197–205.

Koontz, C.W. (1974). *Koontz child developmental programs: Training activities for the first 48 months*. Los Angeles: Western Psychological Services.

Korabek, C.A., Reid, D.H., & Ivancic, M.T. (1981). Improving food intake of profoundly handicapped children through effective supervision of institutional staff. *Applied Research in Mental Retardation, 2*, 68–88.

Lambert, N., Windmiller, M., Tharinger, D., & Cole, L. (1981). *AAMD Adaptive Behavior Scale*. Monterey, CA: CTB/McGraw-Hill.

Lee, L. (1974). *Developmental sentence analyses*. Evanston, IL: Northwestern University Press.

Lentz, F.E. (1982). *An empirical examination of the utility of partial interval and momentary time sampling as measurements of behavior.* Unpublished doctoral dissertation, University of Tennessee, Knoxville.

Liberty, K.A. (1972). *Data decision rules*. Unpublished manuscript, University of Oregon, Regional Resource Center, Eugene.

Liberty, K.A. (1985). Enhancing instruction for maintenance, generalization, and adaptation. In K.C. Lakin & R.H. Bruininks (Eds.), *Strategies for achieving community integration of developmentally disabled citizens* (pp. 29–71). Baltimore: Paul H. Brookes Publishing Co.

Liberty, K.A. (1988). Decision rules and procedures for generalization. In N.G. Haring (Ed.), *Generalization for students with severe handicaps: Strategies and solutions* (pp. 179–204). Seattle: University of Washington Press.

Liberty, K.A., & Billingsley, F.F. (1988). Strategies to improve generalization. In N.G. Haring (Ed.), *Generalization for students with severe handicaps: Strategies and solutions* (pp. 143–176). Seattle: University of Washington Press.

Liberty, K.A., Haring, N.G., White, O.R., & Billingsley, F.F. (1988). A technology for the future: Decision rules for generalization. *Education and Training in Mental Retardation, 23*, 315.

Liberty, K.A., White, O.R., Billingsley, F.F., & Haring, N.G. (1988). Effectiveness of decision rules for generalization. In N.G. Haring (Ed.), *Generalization for students with severe handicaps: Strategies and solutions* (pp. 103–119). Seattle: University of Washington Press.

Lin, C., & Browder, D.M. (1990). An application of engineering principles of motion study for the development of task analyses. *Education and Training in Mental Retardation, 25*, 367–375.

Lindsley, O.R. (1964). Direct measurement and prosthesis of retarded behavior. *Journal of Education, 147*, 60–82.

Lloyd v. Regional Transportation Authority, 548 F. 2d 1277, 1280-84 (F. Cir. 1977).

Lucas, E.A. (1981). *Pragmaticism*. Rockville, MD: Aspen Systems.

MacDonald, J. (1981, January). *ECO taxonomy checklist*. Paper presented at the national conference of The Association for the Severely Handicapped, New York.

MacDonald, J.D. (1985). Communication in autistic persons: Characteristics and intervention. In S.F. Warren & A.K. Rogers-Warren (Eds.), *Teaching functional language: Generalization and maintenance of language skills* (pp. 89–122). Baltimore: University Park Press.

MacDonald, J.D., Gillette, Y., Bickley, M., & Rodriguez, C. (1984). *ECO conversation routines: Models for making everyday activities into language teaching conversations*. Columbus: Ohio State University.

Mace, F.C., & Lalli, J.S. (in press). Linking descriptive and experimental analyses in the treatment of bizarre speech. *Journal of Applied Behavior Analysis*.

Mace, F.M., Lalli, J.S., & Pinter-Lalli, E. (in press). Functional analysis and treatment of aberrant behavior. *Research in Developmental Disabilities*.

Mahoney v. Administrative School District No. 1, 601 P 2nd. (Or. Ct. Appls., 1979).

Markel, G. (1982). Doctoral training in supervision: Meeting an unrecognized but important need. *Teacher Education and Special Education, 5*, 43–50.

Matson, J.L., DiLorenzo, T.M., & Esveldt-Dawson, H. (1981). Independence training as a method of enhancing self help skills acquisition of the mentally retarded. *Behavior Research and Therapy, 19,* 399–405.

McGregor, G., Janssen, C.M., Larsen, L.A., & Tillery, W.L. (1986). Philadelphia's urban model project: A system-wide effort to integrate students with severe handicaps. *Journal of The Association for Persons with Severe Handicaps, 11,* 61–67.

McLean, J.E., & Snyder-McLean, L.K. (1978). *A transactional approach to early language training.* Columbus, OH: Charles E. Merrill.

McLean, J.E., Snyder-McLean, L.K., Sack, S.H., & Decker, D.K. (1982). *A transactional approach to early language: A mediated program.* Columbus, OH: Charles E. Merrill.

Meyer, L.H., Eichinger, J., & Park-Lee, S. (1987). A validation of program quality indicators in educational services for students with severe disabilities. *Journal of The Association for Persons with Severe Handicaps, 12,* 251–263.

Meyer, L.H., & Evans, I.M. (1989). *Nonaversive intervention for behavior problems: A manual for home and community.* Baltimore: Paul H. Brookes Publishing Co.

Meyer, L., Reichle, J., McQuarter, R., Cole, D., Vandercook, T., Evans, I., Neel, R., & Kishi, G. (1985). *Assessment of social competence (ASC): A scale of social competence functions.* Minneapolis: University of Minnesota Consortium Institute for the Education of Severely Handicapped Learners.

Miller, J. (1980). *Assessing language production in children.* Baltimore: University Park Press.

Mithaug, D.E., & Hagmeier, L.D. (1978). The development of procedures to assess prevocational task preference in retarded adults. *AAESPH Review, 3,* 94–115.

Moon, M.S., & Bunker, L. (1987). Recreation and motor skills programming. In M.E. Snell (Ed.), *Systematic instruction of persons with severe handicaps* (3rd ed., pp. 214–244). Columbus, OH: Charles E. Merrill.

Moon, M.S., Goodall, P., Barcus, M., & Brooke, V. (Eds.). (1985). *The supported work model of competitive employment for citizens with severe handicaps: A guide for job trainers.* Richmond: Virginia Commonwealth University, Rehabilitation Research and Training Center.

Moon, M.S., Inge, K.J., Wehman, P., Brooke, V., & Barcus, J.M. (1990). *Helping persons with severe mental retardation get and keep employment: Supported employment strategies and otucomes.* Baltimore: Paul H. Brookes Publishing Co.

Mount, B., & Zwernik, K. (1988). *It's never too early, it's never too late: A booklet about personal futures planning.* St. Paul: Minnesota Governor's Planning Council on Developmental Disabilities.

Mulligan, M., Lacy, L., & Guess, D. (1982). Effects of massed, distributed, and spaced trial sequencing on severely handicapped students' performance. *Journal of The Association for the Severely Handicapped, 7,* 48–61.

Muma, J.R. (1978). *Language handbook: Concepts, assessment, intervention.* Englewood Cliffs, NJ: Prentice-Hall.

Munger, G., Snell, M.E., & Lloyd, B.H. (1989). *How often do you need to collect student data? A study of the effects of frequency of probe data collection and graph characteristics on teachers' visual inferences.* Unpublished manuscript. University of Virginia.

Neel, R.S., & Billingsley, F.F. (1989). *IMPACT: A functional curriculum handbook for students with moderate to severe disabilities.* Baltimore: Paul H. Brookes Publishing Co.

Newton, J.S., Bellamy, G.T., Horner, R.H., Boles, S.M., LeBaron, N.M., & Bennett, A. (1987). Using *The activities catalog* in residential programs for individuals with severe disabilities. In B. Wilcox & G.T. Bellamy, A comprehensive guide to *The activities catalog: An alternative curriculum for youth and adults with severe disabilities* (pp. 125–153). Baltimore: Paul H. Brookes Publishing Co.

Niebel, B.W. (1982). *Motion and time study* (7th ed.). Homewood, IL: Richard D. Irwin.

Oakland, T., & Houchins, S. (1985). A review of the Vineland Adaptive Behavior Scales: Survey. *Journal of Counseling and Development, 63,* 585–586.

O'Brien, J. (1987). A guide to life-style planning. In B. Wilcox, & G.T. Bellamy, A comprehensive guide to *The activities catalog: An alternative curriculum for youth and adults with severe disabilities* (pp. 175–189). Baltimore: Paul H. Brookes Publishing Co.

Page, T.J., Iwata, B.A., & Reid, D.H. (1982). Pyramidal training: A large scale application with institutional staff. *Journal of Applied Behavior Analysis, 15,* 335–351.

Pennsylvania Association for Retarded Citizens v. Commonwealth of Pennsylvania, 343 F. Supp. 279 (E.D. Pa. 1972).

PL 94-142. (1977, August 23). Education of the Handicapped Act of 1975. *Federal Register, 42,* 163.

Powers, M.D., & Handleman, J.S. (1984). *Behavioral assessment of severe development disabilities.* Rockville, MD: Aspen Systems.

Realon, R.E., Lewallen, J.D., & Wheeler, A.J. (1983). Verbal feedback vs. verbal feedback plus praise: The effects on direct care staff's training behaviors. *Mental Retardation, 21,* 209–212.

Renzaglia, A.M., & Bates, P. (1983). Socially appropriate behavior. In M.E. Snell (Ed.), *Systematic instruction of the moderately and severely handicapped* (pp. 314–356). Columbus, OH: Charles E. Merrill.

Repp, A. (1983). *Teaching the mentally retarded.* Englewood Cliffs, NJ: Prentice-Hall.

Repp, A.C., & Deitz, D.E.D. (1979). Improving administrative-related staff behaviors at a state institution. *Mental Retardation, 17,* 185–192.

Risley, R., & Cuvo, A.J. (1980). Training mentally retarded adults to make emergency telephone calls. *Behavior Modification, 4,* 513–525.

Romanczyk, R.G., Kent, R.M., Diament, C., & O'Leary, D.O. (1973). Measuring the reliability of observational data: A reactive process. *Journal of Applied Behavior Analysis, 6,* 175–184.

Rusch, F. (1983). Competitive employment training. In M.E. Snell (Ed.), *Systematic instruction of the moderately and severely handicapped* (pp. 503–520). Columbus, OH: Charles E. Merrill.

Sailor, W., & Guess, D. (1983). *Severely handicapped students: An instructional design.* Boston: Houghton Mifflin.

Sanders, R.M. (1978). *How to plot data.* Lawrence, KS: H & H Enterprises.

Schnorr, R., Ford, A., Davern, L., Park-Lee, S., & Meyer, L. (1989). *The Syracuse curriculum revision manual: A group process for developing a community-referenced curriculum guide.* Baltimore: Paul H. Brookes Publishing Co.

Schoen, S.F. (1986). Assistance procedures to facilitate the transfer of stimulus control: Review and analysis. *Education and Training of the Mentally Retarded, 21,* 62–74.

Shafer, M.S., Rice, M.L., Metzler, H., & Haring, M. (1989). A survey of nondisabled employees' attitudes towards supported employees with mental retardation. *Journal of The Association for Persons with Severe Handicaps, 14,* 137–146.

Shapiro, E.S., & Lentz, F.E., Jr. (1986). Behavioral assessment of academic behavior. In T.R. Kratochwill (Ed.), *Advances in School Psychology, 5,* 87–140.

Shevin, M., & Klein, N.K. (1984). The importance of choice-making skills for students with severe disabilities. *Journal of The Association for the Severely Handicapped, 9*(3), 159–166.

Shoemaker, J., & Reid, D.H. (1980). Decreasing chronic absenteeism among institutional staff: Effects of a low-cost attendance program. *Journal of Organizational Behavior Management, 2,* 317–328.

Sigafoos, J., Cole, D.A., & McQuarter, R. (1987). Current practices in the assessment of students with severe handicaps. *Journal of The Association for Persons with Severe Handicaps, 12,* 264–273.

Snell, M.E. (1978). *Systematic instruction of the moderately and severely handicapped.* Columbus, OH: Charles E. Merrill.

Snell, M.E. (Ed.). (1983). *Systematic instruction of the moderately and severely handicapped* (2nd ed.). Columbus, OH: Charles E. Merrill.

Snell, M.E. (Ed.). (1987). *Systematic instruction of persons with severe handicaps* (3rd ed.). Columbus, OH: Charles E. Merrill.

Snell, M.E., & Browder, D. (1986). Community-referenced instruction: Research and issues. *Journal of The Association for Persons with Severe Handicaps, 11,* 1–11.

Snell, M.E., & Gast, D.L. (1981). Applying delay procedures to the instruction of the severely handicapped. *Journal of The Association for the Severely Handicapped, 5*(4), 3–14.

Snell, M.E., & Grigg, N.C. (1987). Instructional assessment. In M.E. Snell (Ed.), *Systematic instruction of people with severe handicaps,* (3rd ed., pp. 64–109). Columbus, OH: Charles E. Merrill.

Sparrow, S.S., Balla, D.A., & Cicchetti, D.V. (1985). *Vineland Adaptive Behavior Scales.* Circle Pines, MN: American Guidance Service.

Spears, D.L., Rusch, F.R., York, R., & Lilly, M.S. (1981). Training independent arrival behaviors to a severely mentally retarded child. *Journal of The Association for the Severely Handicapped, 6*(2), 40–45.

St. Peter, S.M., Ayres, B.J., Meyer, L., & Park-Lee, S. (1989). Social skills. In A. Ford, R. Schnorr, L. Meyer, L. Davern, J. Black, & P. Dempsey (Eds.), *The Syracuse community-referenced curriculum guide for students with moderate and severe disabilities* (pp. 171–188). Baltimore: Paul H. Brookes Publishing Co.

Stokes, T.F., & Baer, D.M. (1977). An implicit technology of generalization. *Journal of Applied Behavior Analysis, 10,* 349–367.

Stowitschek, J., Stowitschek, C.E., Hendrickson, J.M., & Day, R.M. (1984). *Direct teaching tactics for exceptional children: A practice and supervision guide.* Rockville, MD: Aspen Systems.

Striefel, S., Wetherby, B., & Karlan, G. (1976). Establishing generalized verb-noun instruction-following skills in retarded children. *Journal of Experimental Child Psychology, 22,* 247–260.

Sulzer-Azaroff, B., & Mayer, G.R. (1977). *Applying behavior-analysis procedures for children and youth.* New York: Holt, Rinehart & Winston.

Svinicki, J.G. (1989). Review of the Pyramid Scales. In J.C. Conoley & J.J. Kramer (Eds.), Tenth mental measurements yearbook (pp. 671–673). Lincoln: University of Nebraska Press.

Thvedt, J.E., Zane, T., & Walls, R.T. (1984). Stimulus functions in response chaining. *American Journal of Mental Deficiency, 88,* 661–667.

Touchette, P.E., MacDonald, R.F., & Langer, S.N. (1985). A scatter plot for identifying stimulus control of problem behavior. *Journal of Applied Behavior Analysis, 18*(4), 343–351.

Tucker, J.A. (1985). Curriculum-based assessment: An introduction. *Exceptional Children, 52*(3), 199–204.

Tucker, D.J., & Berry, G.W. (1980). Teaching severely multihandicapped students to put on their own hearing aids. *Journal of Applied Behavior Analysis, 13,* 65–75.

Turnbull, A.P., Barber, P., Behr, S.K., & Kerns, G.M. (1988). The family of children and youth with exceptionalities. In E.L. Meyer & T.M. Skrtic (Eds.), *Exceptional children and youth: An introduction* (3rd ed., pp. 82–107). Denver: Love Publishing Co.

Utley, B.L., Zigmond, N., & Strain, P.S. (1987). How various forms of data affect teacher analysis of student performance. *Exceptional Children, 53,* 411–422.

Uzgiris, I.C., & Hunt, J.M. (1978). *Assessment in infancy: Ordinal scales of psychological development.* Urbana: University of Illinois Press.

van den Pol, R.A., Iwata, B.A., Ivancic, M.T., Page, T.J., Neef, N.A., & Whitely, F.D. (1981). Teaching the handicapped to eat in public places: Acquisition, generalization, and maintenance of restaurant skills. *Journal of Applied Behavior Analysis, 14,* 61–69.

Vandercook, T., York, J., & Forest, M. (1989). The McGill Action Planning System (MAPS): A strategy for building the vision. *Journal of The Association for Persons with Severe Handicaps, 14,* 205–213.

Voeltz, L.M., & Evans, I.M. (1983). Educational validity: Procedures to evaluate outcomes in programs for severely handicapped learners. *Journal of The Association for the Severely Handicapped, 8,* 3–15.

Voeltz, L.M., Wuerch, B.B., & Bockhaut, C.H. (1982). Social validation of leisure activities training with severely handicapped youth. *Journal of The Association for the Severely Handicapped, 7,* 3–13.

Wampold, B.E., & Furlong, N.J. (1981). The heuristics of visual inference. *Behavioral Assessment, 3,* 79–82.

Warren, S.F. (1985). Clinical strategies for the measurement of language generalization. In S.F. Warren & A.K. Rogers-Warren (Eds.), *Teaching functional language: Generalization and maintenance of language skills* (pp. 197–224). Baltimore: University Park Press.

Warren, S.F., & Rogers-Warren, A.K. (1985). *Teaching functional language: An introduction.* In S.F. Warren & A.K. Rogers-Warren (Eds.), *Teaching functional language: Generalization and maintenance of language skills* (pp. 3–23). Baltimore: University Park Press.

Waryas, C.L., & Stremel-Campbell, K. (1978). Grammatical training for the language-delayed child: A new perspective. In R.L. Schiefelbusch (Ed.), *Language intervention strategies* (pp. 145–192). Baltimore: University Park Press.

Wehman, P., Moon, M.S., Everson, J.M., Wood, W., & Barcus, J.M. (1988). *Transition from school to work: New challenges for youth with severe disabilities.* Baltimore: Paul H. Brookes Publishing Co.

Wehman, P., Renzaglia, A., & Bates, P. (1985). *Functional living skills for moderately and severely handicapped individuals.* Austin, TX: PRO-ED.

White, O.R. (1972). *A manual for the calculation and use of the median slope—A technique of progress estimation and prediction in a single case.* Eugene: University of Oregon, Regional Resource Center.

White, O.R. (1980). Adaptive performance objectives: Form versus function. In W. Sailor, B. Wilcox, & L. Brown (Eds.), *Methods of instruction for severely handicapped students* (pp. 47–69). Baltimore: Paul H. Brookes Publishing Co.

White, O.R. (1981). *Making daily classroom decisions.* Paper presented to American Educational Research Association, Los Angeles, CA.

White, O.R. (1985). Aim*star wars: Episodes II and III. *Journal of Precision Teaching, 5,* 86–96.

White, O.R. (1988). Probing skill use. In N.G. Haring (Ed.), *Generalization for students with severe handicaps: Strategies and solutions* (pp. 129–142). Seattle: University of Washington Press.

White, O.R., & Haring, N.G. (1980). *Exceptional teaching.* Columbus, OH: Charles E. Merrill.

Whyte, R.A., Van Houten, R., & Hunter, W. (1983). The effects of public posting on teachers' performance of supervision duties. *Education and Treatment of Children, 6,* 21–28.

Wilcox, B., & Bellamy, G.T. (1987a). *The activities catalog: An alternative curriculum for youth and adults with severe disabilities.* Baltimore: Paul H. Brookes Publishing Co.

Wilcox, B., & Bellamy, G.T. (1987b). A comprehensive guide to *The activities catalog: An alternative curriculum for youth and adults with severe disabilities.* Baltimore: Paul H. Brookes Publishing Co.

Williams, G.E., & Cuvo, A.J. (1986). Training apartment upkeep skills to rehabilitation clients: A comparison of task analytic strategies. *Journal of Applied Behavior Analysis, 19,* 39–51.

Wolf, M.M. (1978). Social validity: The case for subjective measurement, or how applied behavior analysis is finding its heart. *Journal of Applied Behavior Analysis, 11,* 203–214.

Wolfensberger, W. (1972). *The principle of normalization in human services.* Toronto: National Institute of Mental Retardation.

Wuerch, B.B., & Voeltz, L.M. (1982). *Longitudinal Leisure skills for severely handicapped learners: The Ho'onanea curriculum component.* Baltimore: Paul H. Brookes Publishing Co.

INDEX

AAMD Adaptive Behavior Scale, 42–43, 68
ABC analysis, 256–258, 259
ABCD objective, 66
ABI *see* Adaptive Behavior Inventory
Academic skills, 213–214, 241, 243, 244
Acquisition phase of learning, 103
  generalization and, 301, 302
  problem with, definition of, 128
Activities
  functional, fine motor skills and, 234, 236
  see also specific type
Activities Catalog, 41, 157
Adaptations, simplification of responses with, 83–84, 86
Adaptive Behavior Inventory (ABI), 39, 42–43, 68
Adaptive behavior scales, 5–6, 38–39
  addresses for obtainment of, 68
  comparison of, 42–43
  skills assessed by, 40
  see also specific scale
Adaptive responses, limited, vocational assessment and, 197–198
Age, vocational assessment and, 181
Ambulation, 236, 239
  goal-directed, 237, 239
American Sign Language, syntax in, 222
Anecdotal assessment of interfering behavior, 256–259
Annual assessment, 21, 27, 59–67
  case study of, 61, 65
  forms for, 371–377
  of routines, 133–135
  of specific skill data, 129–130
  steps for, 59–61, 62–64
  and writing objectives for first-year plan, 65–66
Antecedents-Behavior-Consequences (ABC) analysis, 256–258, 259

Applied behavioral psychology model of behavioral assessment, 10–11, 17
Applied behavior analysis, 7
  ongoing assessment and, 70
  see also Ongoing assessment
Armstrong v. Kline, 299
ASC, *see* Assessment of Social Competence
Assessment
  defined, 1
  educational, 1–25
    see also Educational assessment
  see also specific assessment tools; specific type of assessment
Assessment of Social Competence (ASC): A Scale of Competence Functions, 249–250
Assessment plan, *see* Data-based supervision; Supervisors, assessment plan for
Attention, motivation and, task analytic assessment and, 89
Attitude-and-information survey, in ecological inventory, 37
Autonomy, 1–2
  skills in, 137

Balthazar Scales of Adaptive Behavior, 42–43, 68
Battle v. Commonwealth, 299
Behavior(s)
  chain of, *see* Response(s), chain of
  deviant, levels of, 254, 255
  function of, 16, 257–258, 259
  pivotal, generalized responsivity and, 293–295
  problem, *see* Interfering behavior; Problem behavior
  public, 206, 207
  target, 10–11
Behavior management techniques, observation of, 325–327, 328–329